SNACKABLES

for

SPIRITUAL GROWTH

Kennith C. Gray

ISBN: 978-1-9994009-1-0

DEDICATION

I dedicate this book to my children Naomi, Noah and Noelle, in the hope that as I have set a course for our family to follow Christ, that they too will walk in the knowledge of Christ and His unfailing love.

My prayer is that they will always trust in God's plan for their lives, even if things seem unfair, difficult or painful.

I declare my love for all three of God's blessings to me and I'm honoured to have children as blessed, anointed, intelligent and talented as they are.

I leave this first book as a spiritual heritage and pray it will be a true blessing.

Lastly, I dedicate these writings to my future grandchildren that have yet to be born, but whom God already knows and will bring forth in His timing and for His purposes.

I declare **Psalm 112:2** (NLT) over my children and all generations that follow:

> *Their children will be successful everywhere; an entire generation of godly people will be blessed.*

FOREWORD

In the year 2000, just two years into the Faith, and a new father, one of my favourite scriptures was:

> *A good man leaves an inheritance to his children's children, and the wealth of the sinner is stored up for [the hands of] the righteous.*
>
> - **Proverbs 13:22** *(AMP)*

Since then, experience and the Word have taught me that one cannot be good, or righteous, or change the fleshly nature and conform *themselves* to the image of Christ. It takes the help of the Holy Spirit, continuously working to transform us. Our role is to seek first the Kingdom of God, to do the things that *allow* His Spirit to grow and do its work in us.

Circumstances may make it seem impossible, but God reminds us that we "overcome by the Blood of the lamb and the word of our testimony." In His word, God tells us, through His messenger Paul, "we can do all things through Christ who strengthens us." He says, His Word is bread and life and that His Holy Spirit is living water.

For anything to grow it must be fed. Contained within the pages of this book is bread (the Word) and water (Spiritual insights) in practical, bite-sized, topic-based, nuggets called "snackables".

I pray that as you read, meditate and put into practice daily, the wisdom and knowledge found within His Word and within this book, that you will grow spiritually and have testimony upon testimony, victory upon victory.

With love in Christ,

Kennith C. Gray

TABLE OF CONTENTS

PHYSICALLY FIT BUT SPIRITUALLY MALNOURISHED?

Psalm 34:8 (NKJV)

> *Oh, taste and see that the Lord is good; Blessed is the man who trusts in Him!*

Isaiah 55:1-2 (NKJV)

> *(1) Ho! Everyone who thirsts, come to the waters; And you who have no money, Come, buy and eat. Yes, come, buy wine and milk without money and without price.*
>
> *(2) Why do you [weigh out silver] spend money for what is not bread, and your wages for what does not satisfy? Listen carefully to Me, and eat what is good, and let your soul delight itself in abundance.*

I have had this message in my spirit for a few years now, as I have observed the health and wellness industry explode and the clothing of women diminish. It's clear that the focus of many, both men and women, in and out of the church, is how "sexy" they look. From anti-aging creams to youth serums, people spend much time and money on living a longer life and yet the most they can hope to achieve is 120 years (Genesis 6:3). Little to no thought is taken for the things of God and eternity.

Don't get me wrong, I believe it's important to take care of yourself, but more care should be given to your spirit. Here is what Jesus said to the Pharisees who were taking great pride on their outward appearance and neglecting their inner beings.

Matthew 23:27-28 (NKJV)

> *(27) Woe to you, scribes and Pharisees, hypocrites! For you are like whitewashed tombs which indeed appear **beautiful outwardly,** but inside are full of dead men's bones and all uncleanness.*

> *(28) Even so you also outwardly appear righteous to men, but **inside you are full of hypocrisy and lawlessness.***

Harsh words, from a loving savour, but the point I want to impress upon you is that, as God's creation, we are three-part beings – mind, body and spirit.

If you exercise your body and enjoy the temporary "high" you get from increased endorphins, you should also exercise your spirit and see how much higher the Lord will take you and how much longer He will sustain you.

In my experience, the effects of prayer, fasting, worship and the Word are longer lasting.

In fact, there is a long list of benefits to exercising your spirit; your entire being is helped. Fears, depression and anxiety vanish. Pain and sickness disappear, and your soul rejoices. You are happier, and stresses don't stress you. Many testify of the Lord's blessings in situations that seemed impossible:

- Financial breakthroughs
- Family curses broken

- Loneliness gone, even without a life partner
- Children become obedient (I know, right?!)
- Employment gained
- Cancer and other chronic diseases are healed
- People who mistreated you have a change of heart

As you come into alignment spiritually, you are cleansed from all unrighteousness and the enemies that fight against your life, have no choice but to flee.

As a side-benefit, exercising your spirit does not require a gym membership. You can build your spirit any time and any place.

You don't have to have the right equipment; whenever you need help or direction from the Lord (for me that's almost always) just call out to Him and He's there to lift you up and point you in the right direction.

Finally, my dear brothers and sisters consider this:

> No matter how hard you work out in the gym or how
> well you eat, eventually your body will grow old and
> die; but if you keep your spirit in tune, you will receive a
> new, glorified (perfected) body when Jesus returns.
> Shout Hallelujah!!

Task: Read all of Psalm 34 and Isaiah 55 and rejoice! Honour God in your day. Don't be as the hypocrites who take care of their outward appearance, but neglect feeding their spirit with the good things of God. Trust me. Your soul will thank you for it, now and in eternity.

FAINT NOT

Galatians 6:9

> _And let us not be weary in well doing: for in due season
> we shall reap, if we faint not._

Like Mona Lisa's smile, this verse of scripture lands smack-dab in the middle of a masterful and wonderful letter to the church in Galatia.

Paul paints a glorious picture of how we should walk as believers. That we should be humble, bear one another's burdens, work diligently on our own burdens, have patience as we sow in the spirit, so as not to be bound by religion. Remaining free, because of the work Jesus did on the cross.

Sow into your spirit, through Prayer, Fasting, Worship and the Word; which are the four pillars of our spiritual houses.

Paul is encouraging us, not to grow faint when building our spiritual houses, so we'll reap in due season.

Thank you, Jesus, for the Apostle Paul!!!

Prayer: Lord, teach me to pray without ceasing, and fast periodically so that I may reap in my spirit all that you have planted. Lord, fill my heart with joy and thankfulness that I may worship you in spirit and in truth. Holy Spirit, create in me a hunger for more of the Word and show me the mysteries of Christ. Amen.

FEAR NOT

Isaiah 41:10 *(NKJV)*

> *Fear not, for I am with you; Be not dismayed, for I am your God. I will strengthen you, Yes, I will help you, I will uphold you with My righteous right hand.*

It has been said that "fear not" is recorded 365 times in the Bible – one for each day of the year. But, so what?

Simply telling someone to fear not, man-up, get over it, stop being a scaredy-cat, and so on, is not enough to allay fears.

When children have bad dreams, what do they do? They go to their father and mother's bedroom for safety and comfort. Just like children who know their parents will be there for them, we need to know that our **God is there for us**.

- If your cupboards are looking bare, He says "I am Jehovah Jireh your provider"
- If you need healing in your body, He is Jehovah Rapha
- If you're not sure which direction to go, He is a lamp unto your feet
- If you're having problems with your children, He says "I will turn the hearts of the children back to their fathers"
- If you feel you're not smart enough, He says "if anyone lacks wisdom, let him ask of God"
- If you are afraid of death, He says "fear not, for I will raise you up just like I raised up my son Jesus"
- If there is sin in your life, He says "I am your redeemer"
- If you feel unloved and alone, He says "perfect love casts out fear and that he'll never leave you nor forsake you"

- If you are depressed, He says "I have given you a sound mind"

- If you feel powerless, He says "they that know their God will do exploits" – hallelujah!

In summary, we don't have to fear anything or anyone when we KNOW OUR GOD. Aren't you glad you know God?

Prayer: Lord, I thank you for revealing yourself to me. Today if/when I'm faced with fear, I will run to you in prayer because you are my refuge, my redeemer and in you, I find strength. I want to know you more, for you are a very present help in a time of trouble, a friend to the friendless and hope to the hopeless. Thank you, Jesus, for being my all in all. Amen.

BELIEF

Mark 9:23-25 *(NLT)*

> *(23) "What do you mean, 'If I can'?" Jesus asked. "Anything is possible if a person believes."*
>
> *(24) The father instantly cried out, "I do believe, but help me overcome my unbelief!"*
>
> *(25) When Jesus saw that the crowd of onlookers was growing, he rebuked the evil spirit. "Listen, you spirit that makes this boy unable to hear and speak," he said. "I command you to come out of this child and never enter him again!"*

This passage excerpt comes at a time when Jesus' disciples already had success in casting out demons and healing the sick. However, in this case, because of unbelief, they were unable to free the demon-possessed boy, so the father now complains to Jesus.

I love Jesus' response when the father asks if Jesus can heal the boy.

I'll paraphrase…

> *Are you serious? Of course, I can, because anything is possible when a person believes.*

I equally like the father's response…"I do believe, help my unbelief."

Many Christians are satisfied with their level of belief (or unbelief) and remain stuck in their abilities or worse, their troubles. I'm not satisfied…how about you?

Prayer: Lord, today when my unbelief hinders your work in me, and the world around me, step in and remind me that all things are possible if I believe. Lord uproot every hidden place in me that conceals my unbelief that I may do greater works as you've promised. Amen!

BEING SPIRIT-LED

Matthew 4:1-4 (NLT)

> *(1) Then Jesus was led by the Spirit into the wilderness to be tempted there by the devil.*
>
> *(2) For forty days and forty nights he fasted and became very hungry.*
>
> *(3) During that time the devil came and said to him, "If you are the Son of God, tell these stones to become loaves of bread."*
>
> *(4) But Jesus told him, "No! The Scriptures say, 'People do not live by bread alone, but by every word that comes from the mouth of God.'"*

Satan and his agents will talk a lot of things into your ears; "hate this person", "tell this lie", "gossip about that minister or sister", "life is not worth living", "speak this negative word over your life", and so on – but we must listen to the Holy Spirit and God's Word.

God's Word says, that He loves us, died for us, desires to talk with us, commune with us, and that He only wants the best for us.

He's a good God.

Prayer: Father God, thank you for the Holy Spirit that guides me into all truth. I cover my ears and anoint my tongue with the blood of Jesus, so the enemy will not have any legal hold on my destiny. I will NOT give Satan any authority by listening to him and his lies. I choose to follow your lead and listen to your instructions. Amen.

UNITY

Psalm 133

> *(1) Behold, how good and how pleasant it is for brethren to dwell together in unity!*
>
> *(2) It is like the precious ointment upon the head that ran down upon the beard, even Aaron's beard: that went down to the skirts of his garments;*
>
> *(3) As the dew of Hermon, and as the dew that descended upon the mountains of Zion: for there the Lord commanded the blessing, even life for evermore.*

Notice how King David compares unity to a precious ointment that **flows** and how it's a blessing and even life for evermore. Jesus instructed us to settle any disputes with others before bringing an offering unto the Lord (**Matthew 5:23-25**).

In Acts, it is recorded many times that they were together in "one accord". Lastly, even Jesus prayed that we would be "one" just as He and the Father are one (**John 17:20-23**).

I encourage you to let unity flow, so that your anointing will break every yoke and bring you and others into life eternal.

Prayer: Lord, today as far as it is up to me, I will live at peace with others. Lord, I will esteem others, and not allow pride and envy to overrule the love you've placed in my heart. Thank you, Jesus, for the victory and the blessings! Amen.

HONOUR

1 Samuel 2:30 *(NKJV)*

> *Therefore, the Lord God of Israel says: 'I said indeed that your house and the house of your father would walk before Me forever.' But now the Lord says: 'Far be it from Me; for **those who honour Me I will honour, and those who despise Me shall be lightly esteemed.***

Since, God is the same yesterday, today and forever, we need to walk humbly and in reverence (with respect) to God and give Him Honour.

I looked up some synonyms of the word "honour" and these three stood out for me; **praise**, **worship** and **exaltation**.

The Bible says that Jesus has been exalted and given a name that is above every name. So today, let every breath you take, and everything you do, give Him honour, praise and worship.

Prayer: Lord, thank you! I give you praise and I say you are my God in whom I will trust. You are holy and worthy of my worship. Lord, have your way in my life. Take control and lead me down the path of righteousness, that I may live to honour you in all that I do. Amen!

Application: Now from your own lips, bless the Lord until you can think of nothing else to praise Him for.

REST

Matthew 11:28-30

> *(28) Come unto me, all ye that labour and are heavy laden, and I will give you rest.*
>
> *(29) Take my yoke upon you and learn of me; for I am meek and lowly in heart: and ye shall find rest unto your souls.*
>
> *(30) For my yoke is easy, and my burden is light.*

Most weekends tend to be busy for me, especially after putting in a full week of 9-5 and a bit of extra time.

However, when the Lord put this scripture into my spirit, it couldn't be more applicable. I need to rest more. Looking closer, Jesus wasn't talking about the sleep type of rest, but rest for our souls. Notice He also says, "learn of me".

If I've learned anything about Jesus, it is that He would often get away from the crowd and go up into a mountain or quiet place to pray and be refreshed. What about you?

Life is filled with stresses; more work than week; more month than money; keeping the kids fed; getting the bills paid; driving kids to programs…fill in the blank of whatever it is that keeps you from resting and you get the idea.

Our minds are constantly thinking of the next task or activity. Let me add one more to your list; pray.

Application: Take some time to just meditate on Jesus and learn of Him. Block everything out – put on headphones, find a closet and just hide out with God. Take as long as you need, in order to find peace and rest for your soul.

LIFE

John 10:10 *(NKJV)*

> *The thief does not come except to steal, and to kill, and to destroy. I have come that they may have life, and that they may have it more abundantly.*

Whenever, this scripture is quoted, Satan is most often identified as the thief. However, if you look at the context and "listen" to what Jesus is really saying you will see a few thieves identified. I believe Jesus is teaching us that **anyone (see verses 8, 12, 13) or any religion (see verse 1) that doesn't point you to Him, as the way to eternal life, is a thief**.

In verse 7, Jesus says, "I am the door of the sheep" – notice he says THE DOOR – definite article and not "a door". There is no other way into the Kingdom of God or eternal life.

Be confident in knowing that if you are a born-again Christian, you have entered in the right door.

Prayer: Jesus, thank you for making the way to life clear. Help me to be a witness to those that are being robbed of life and destroyed through lack of knowledge. I will forever be careful to give you all the glory. Amen.

ESCAPING TEMPTATION

1 Corinthians 10:13 (NLT)

> *The temptations in your life are no different from what others experience. And God is faithful. He will not allow the temptation to be more than you can stand. When you are tempted, he will show you a way out so that you can endure.*

Tye Tribbett has a song titled "Victory", in which he quotes this verse and explains "that in every building there must be an exit sign, so it is with temptation." Now, temptation isn't just sexual lust, it's **anything that has influence over you to live outside of God's best for you**.

But notice above, it says "God is faithful", and remember the Lord's prayer "lead us not into temptation"? We don't have to use our will power. God will show us our way of escape if we're in communication with Him, ask Him to guide us and allow Him to have His way.

Prayer: Heavenly Father, today when I'm tempted to curse the driver who cuts me off; or drives too slow; today Lord if I try to hold onto bitterness or behave in any way the doesn't please you; please show me the "EXIT sign" and my way of escape. I desire to walk perfect before you. Father, teach me how to live righteously and not tread lightly on (take for granted) the blood of Jesus that saved me. Amen.

NEW TESTAMENT

Luke 22:20

> *Likewise, also the cup after supper, saying,* this cup is the new testament in my blood, which is shed for you.

These words spoken by Jesus at the "last supper" are very significant to understanding why and what happened when Jesus went to the cross. A few synonyms of the word testament are, **proof**, **covenant** and **evidence** which I'll use to clarify two points. **First**, the strongest covenant or promise that can be made between two parties will always include the shedding of blood. In fact, in some cultures, to prove the bride was a virgin, the groom presents the blood-stained bedsheet as evidence. **Secondly**, the scriptures say that under the law (old covenant), "there is no remission of sin without the shedding of blood" (paraphrased **Hebrews 9:22**).

So, when Jesus said these words, what he was essentially saying was, I'll remove your sin once and for all – no more law or sheep sacrifices (old covenant) – I'm doing a new thing, and no one can deny or undo it. Remember that!

Prayer: Jesus, thank you for shedding your blood. I promise to remember what you've done for me. I accept your sacrifice and I too present my body as a living testament to your finished work on the cross. I choose to live a life that honours your sacrifice.

PRAYER

Luke 6:12 *(God's Word Translation)*

> *At that time Jesus went to a mountain to pray. He spent the whole night in prayer to God.*

Well it's confession time again…sigh. As much as I like to pray nowadays, I must admit, it took me many years to even think it was important. I figured, faith was enough.

I felt I was too busy and didn't need to waste time praying, especially since God knows everything. I felt 10 minutes should be enough.

However, that's not what we see in scripture. **Notice Jesus prayed ALL NIGHT!** I'm sure it wasn't the first time and it wasn't His last.

With depression and increased stresses on our lives, now more than ever, we need to up the ante on prayer.

In the Bible, prayer freed Peter from prison, prayer raised Lazarus, prayer multiplied the fish and bread, prayer helped Jesus surrender His will in the garden, and it was prayer, offered to God, when Jesus breathed his last breath…Father into your hands I commit my spirit.

Application: PRAY! No matter how you do it, no matter how long, just talk to God. Tell him how you're feeling. Don't bring him a laundry list of wants, just talk to Him about what His plans are for you. Thank Him for all He has done for you.

If you run out of things to say, tell him "thank you" *about a million times* – He doesn't get tired of worship. If you get tired of saying thank you, pray in tongues (the heavenly language) and let the Holy Spirit make intercession for you.

As we mature, 1 hour (minimum) of prayer each day is our goal.

JOY

Romans 14:17 *(NLT)*

> *For the Kingdom of God is not a matter of what we eat or drink, but of living a life of goodness and peace and joy in the Holy Spirit.*

In this chapter of Romans, the Apostle Paul, is advising Christians (most likely Jewish) not to put down or make other Christians (most likely Gentiles or Romans) feel guilty because they eat things, that in Levitical Law, God had called unclean or sinful. In verse 17, Paul tells them what the Kingdom really is.

So, what is JOY in the Holy Spirit or Holy Ghost?

For several years as a believer, I wasn't very happy. I often teased myself saying, that I would be the first "angry" pastor if I ever started a church. Then, one day while kneeling and praying bedside, it happened; the Holy Spirit visited me just like Jesus said He would. It felt like I was a disciple on the Day of Pentecost.

I didn't understand it then, but now that I'm looking back, the greatest emotion I experienced was JOY as tears ran down my face and spiritual words flowed out of my mouth from the depth of my being. Hallelujah!

Here is one of Jesus' promises from ***John 16:22*** *(NKJV)*

> *Therefore, you now have sorrow; but I will see you again and your heart will rejoice, and your joy no one will take from you.*

Prayer: Jesus, you said you would pour out your spirit on all flesh and that your Holy Spirit would be a comfort to me. Jesus, I thank you for truth and desire this gift of joy. Please fill me with joy as I worship you. [now love on Jesus for the next 30 minutes expecting a change]

OBEDIENCE

***1 Samuel 15:22-23** (NLT)*

> *(22) But Samuel replied, "What is more pleasing to the LORD: your burnt offerings and sacrifices or your obedience to his voice? Listen! Obedience is better than sacrifice, and submission is better than offering the fat of rams.*

> *(23) Rebellion is as sinful as witchcraft, and stubbornness as bad as worshiping idols. So because you have rejected the command of the LORD, he has rejected you as king."*

How many times have you heard the quote "**obedience is better than sacrifice**"? Do you know the context in which Samuel spoke those words? In verse 3 of the chapter, Saul was instructed by the Lord to completely destroy the Amalekite nation for opposing God's people. Saul destroyed everything except the good stuff and kept king Agag alive, sort of like a Trophy for bragging rights.

As believers, we can be like that too. We'll give up the really bad things, but the things we enjoy – or the things that we like to boast about - those things we won't change, even if God says so (ahem, been there, done that). God is not a half-way god, and to Him, **partial obedience is still disobedience**. God sees disobedience as rejecting His commands and thus He rejected Saul as king and began to seek another.

Prayer: Father, I know I've been disobedient even if only partially. Please forgive me. Holy Spirit, help me to hear more clearly and trust the Father's voice completely. Amen.

ALL IN 'TILL THE END

Luke 9:62 *(NLT)*

> *But Jesus told him,* "Anyone who puts a hand to the plow and then looks back is not fit for the Kingdom of God."

If you've ever questioned, doubted and turned away from God, you know how awful it feels and how hard it is to come back (me too).

In fact, in **Hebrews 6:4** *(NLT)* the writer says,

> *For it is impossible to bring back to repentance those who were once enlightened—those who have experienced the good things of heaven and shared in the Holy Spirit.*

Thankfully the chapter doesn't end there, so the next time you feel you can't do this Christian thing, remember the writer's remarks in **Hebrews 6:9-12** *(NLT)*

> *(9) Dear friends, even though we are talking this way, we really don't believe it applies to you. We are confident that **you are meant for better things**, things that come with salvation.*

> *(10) For **God is not unjust**. He will not forget how hard you have worked for him...*

> *(11) ...keep on loving others as long as life lasts, in order to make certain that what you hope for will come true.*

> *(12) Then **you will not become spiritually dull** and indifferent. Instead, you will follow the example of those who are going to **inherit God's promises** because of their **faith and endurance**.*

You see, **no one can convince you or bring you back to faith, but you**. *You* must commit once again, to give your ALL to Jesus.

Without looking back, press forward in Christ, so you will win the race. The only way He won't accept you, is if you reject the leading of His Holy Spirit and stop coming back to Him.

Prayer: Lord, I commit to following in your footsteps today, tomorrow and forever. Protect my mind with the helmet of salvation so the enemy can't confuse me. I will renew my mind and grow spiritually by feasting – or snacking ☺ – on your Word. Thank you, Jesus, for never leaving or forsaking me. Amen!

YOU HAVE AUTHORITY

Luke 10:19 (NLT)

> *"Look, I have given you authority over all the power of the enemy, and you can walk among snakes and scorpions and crush them. Nothing will injure you."*

Do not wait for life to hand you your victory, or bury you. Grab hold of your destiny and act with authority; Jesus has already given it to you.

Prayer & Declarations: Lord, I receive your Word and power. Thank you. I am strong. I am rich. I have all that I need as it pertains to life and godliness. I am blessed and highly favoured. Amen!

EVANGELISM

Luke 2:29-32 *(NLT)*

> *(29) "Sovereign Lord, now let your servant die in peace, as you have promised.*
>
> *(30) I have seen your salvation,*
>
> *(31) which you have prepared for all people.*
>
> *(32) He is a light to reveal God to the nations, and he is the glory of your people Israel!"*

The verses above were spoken by Simeon, a priest, who prophesied about Jesus who was sent by God to save the world.

Later in **Luke 4:43,** Jesus confirms his calling and would eventually complete His assignment.

Before His betrayal and arrest in the Garden, Jesus prays for His disciples (**John 17**) and passes them the "evangelism torch" (**John 17:18** As thou hast sent me into the world, even so have I also sent them into the world.).

Lastly when Jesus is about to ascend into heaven, He gives the Great Commission to His disciples as a final reminder (**Matthew 28:18-20**).

Now more than ever we need to remember our assignment.

Prayer: Lord, show me who you want me to reach with your love and truth. Jesus, open the conversation with those who are ready to receive your wonderful grace today.

GIFTS

1 Corinthians 12:27-28 *(NLT)*

> *(27) All of you together are Christ's body, and each of you is a part of it.*
>
> *(28) Here are some of the parts God has appointed for the church:*
>
> *first are apostles, second are prophets, third are teachers, then those who do miracles, those who have the gift of healing, those who can help others, those who have the gift of leadership, those who speak in unknown languages. [I'll add, including the heavenly language]*

I know you've probably heard a million sermons on this passage of scripture, but I want to reinforce the following.

1. Notice that it is God who gives the gifts.
2. Notice also, gifts are given for a purpose.

In another scripture, it says gifts are given according to the measure of faith. Why?

Putting it all together, I believe God gives gifts so they can be used to help others, and it is your "measure of faith" that determines whether you will use a particular gift.

The gifts God gives, reflects our life's purpose, but we're to use them faithfully for His purposes. In doing so, we find fulfillment.

Prayer: God, show me how my gifts connect with the purpose for which you've created me. Place me in places where I can use my gifts to bless someone and show them your goodness and love. Amen.

LOVE

1 Corinthians 12:31 *(NLT)*

> *So, you should earnestly desire the most helpful gifts. But now let me show you a way of life that is best of all.*

1 Corinthians 13:1 *(NLT)*

> *If I could speak all the languages of earth and of angels, but didn't love others, I would only be a noisy gong or a clanging cymbal.*

Previously, I spoke about gifts, their importance and their purposes. Continuing Paul's message, he shows us that another more precious gift, is the gift of love.

Love is why God sent His son Jesus, and why Jesus took our sins to the cross, paying, in full, the penalty, and brought peace between us, and God.

Love is a foundational key to the kingdom of God. Love is who God is and we are created in His image. As His image bearers, we are to imitate and exemplify His love.

Prayer: Lord, keep me in remembrance of who you are, why you came and what you've done.

Holy Spirit, teach me how to love as Christ loves. Jesus, as you were moved with compassion, I commit today to act with compassion. I will smile and acknowledge those around me, for you bring me great joy.

Thank you for loving me enough to pay the price of sin. Amen.

GIVE GRACE TO ONE ANOTHER

Ephesians 4:29

> *Let no corrupt communication proceed out of your mouth, but that which is good to the use of edifying, that it may minister grace unto the hearers.*

Colossians 4:5-6

> *(5) Walk in wisdom toward them that are without, redeeming the time.*
>
> *(6) Let your speech be always with grace, seasoned with salt, that ye may know how ye ought to answer every man.*

1 Thessalonians 5:11

> *Wherefore comfort yourselves together, and edify one another, even as also ye do.*

I once led a Thursday Bible Study group that did this very well. In fact, I want to thank sisters Claudette, Holly, Sally, Karen, Joy and many others for the encouragement as I stepped out in faith to start my ministry.

I encourage you, the reader, to uplift and share a kind word with those you know…especially your spouses and children. Give grace as we've also received His grace.

Prayer: Lord Jesus, your Word says, "out of the abundance of the heart, the mouth speaks", so I ask you to fill my heart abundantly with the joy and gladness that comes with knowing your love. Holy Spirit with gladness in my heart, I ask you to take complete control of my tongue today. I ask that you make my words graceful to those I encounter and that they will want to know you personally. Amen.

FAITH

Hebrews 11:1

> *Now faith is the substance of things hoped for, the evidence of things not seen.*

Many people confuse hope with faith, so I thought I'd help a few people out with this little anecdote.

You know you've gone beyond hope and into faith when you move or take action toward that which you hope for.

The Bible says, without faith it is impossible to please God and the question I asked was, "why?"

The response was "faith without works is dead and you serve the living God and the God of the living."

You can't say you are **walking** in faith if you're not actually doing anything or going anywhere.

Prayer: Lord Jesus, today I take a step of faith in the thing which I'm hoping for. Please order my steps, so that I do not stumble along in my journey. Give me the courage of David to walk through the valley and the fortitude of Caleb, to climb the mountain for my victory. Amen!

COMPLETENESS

Luke 4:40

> *Now when the sun was setting, **all** they that had **any** sick with diverse diseases brought them unto him; and he laid his hands on **every one** of them and healed them.*

Notice how the writer, uses *"all"*, *"any"* and *"every one"* to thoroughly describe a magnificent healing event? Jesus is not a half-way God, He finishes what He starts. In John 17:4, Jesus says, "I have finished the work you have given me to do."

The truth is, we are living in the finished work from the cross. In fact, those were Jesus' last words as He died to pay for our sins – "it is finished" translated from the Greek word "tetelestai" which means paid in full.

There is nothing left to do, except believe that He's done it. Do you believe? Even if you're not sure, repeat this until you do:

Declarations: As I work out my salvation, I declare and believe that the Lord, who has begun a good thing in me, will leave nothing undone. I declare complete healing in my entire body and in those I love. I believe that the Lord keeps me from any of the enemy's traps and attacks. I am covered by the blood of Jesus, and I confidently fulfill every one of Jesus' commandments and share His gospel with everyone from all nations. Amen!

DON'T BE MERCHANDISE

2 Peter 2:1-3

> *(1) But there were false prophets also among the people, even as there shall be false teachers among you, who privily shall bring in damnable heresies, even denying the Lord that bought them, and bring upon themselves swift destruction.*

> *(2) And many shall follow their pernicious ways; by reason of whom the way of truth shall be evil spoken of.*

> *(3) And through covetousness shall they with feigned words make merchandise of you: whose judgment now of a long time lingereth not, and their damnation slumbereth not.*

The other day, I came across a website run by a non-believer who charges Christians to have other Christians pray for each other. He has probably made over one million dollars beguiling people – prayer, healing and the Word were all given to us freely. It's a shame we feel we have to buy God's gifts. We should know better. So, my advice to you is, **don't be merchandise**. Don't just blindly follow those that say they are of God, or give of your resources without first testing spirits to discern which is truth, and which is false. The Apostle Paul says to study and show yourself approved of God, rightly dividing the Word of truth.

Prayer: Holy Spirit, grant me insight into the spirit realm and discernment that I may know truth from falsehood. Lord, open the eyes of my understanding that I may see clearly and only follow after you. Lord Jesus, I thank you for sending the Holy Spirit who guides me into all truth. Amen!

SPEAK THE WORD

Matthew 8:8-9

> *(8) The centurion answered and said, Lord, I am not worthy that thou shouldest come under my roof: but **speak the word only**, and my servant shall be healed.*
>
> *(9) For I am a man under authority, having soldiers under me: and I say to this man, Go, and he goeth; and to another, Come, and he cometh; and to my servant, Do this, and he doeth it.*

The centurion, who understood authority, knew that Jesus only needed to "speak the Word" and the sickness would have to obey. The reason sickness must obey is because disease is a condition of the spirit and all spirits understand and bow down to Jesus' authority. Read the snackable on "You Have Authority" and the one on "Restoration"; meditate and understand authority and begin to speak God's Word over every disease. It not only works for healing sicknesses, but all manner of oppression, depression and living a godly life. Become a speaker of His Word and watch what God will do.

Prayer: Father, you are not a man that you can lie, so I stand on your Word that is settled in heaven. Your son, Jesus, said he has given me power to trample on serpents and so now in the authority of that word I speak over everyone reading this, that they will prosper in health, in finances, in relationships with man/woman and with you. They will no longer be deceived by the devil, for your Holy Spirit will expose him and his agents. Thank you, Father, for I know you always hear me. Amen!

DO THE WORD

James 1:22

> *But be ye doers of the word, and not hearers only, deceiving your own selves.*

I encourage you to read or better yet, **assimilate** (next snackable) the entire first chapter of James. It's a good one! I know it has helped me with bridling my tongue – verse 26.

Also, when I'm not sure what "to do", I read Matthew chapter 5 and pick something. Or I scour the book of Acts of the Apostles. I always find something that I'm not doing quite right.

By the way, if you're getting into and reading/studying the Word, that too is *doing* the Word.

Stay blessed and remember what James said; if we are only hearers of the Word, we're only fooling ourselves.

Prayer: Father, thank you for your grace to walk in your truth. I commit today to be a doer of your Word. I will help the helpless, I will speak goodness and I will remember who I am in you, and be a better witness for your son Jesus the Christ. Amen.

ASSIMILATE THE WORD

Joshua 1:8

> *This book of the law shall not depart out of thy mouth;
> but thou shalt **meditate therein day and night**, that
> thou mayest **observe to do** according to all that is
> written therein: for then thou shalt make thy way
> prosperous, and then thou shalt have good success.*

Psalm 1:2

> *But his delight is in the law of the Lord; and in his law
> doth he **meditate day and night**.*

Although the scriptures above are about meditating the Word, I wanted to share another tip I learned from Gary Carpenter about studying the Bible, called assimilation.

Remember this sitcom song?

> *"Just sit right back and you'll hear a tale,*
> *A tale of a fateful trip*
> *That started from this tropic port*
> *Aboard this tiny ship."*

Ahem – you can stop singing now. 😊

I know I'm dating myself, but it's from Gilligan's Island and if you remembered it before you got to the 3rd line, it's because you were **faithful** to watching the show **day-in and day-out repeatedly.** You didn't have to *try* and remember it…it just happened.

Assimilating the Word is simply that, **repetition**; reading a single chapter or small book in the Bible over and over – back-to-back each day. For example, in December 2013, I read the book of

Ephesians 10 times – my goal was 30 – I'm a slow reader – but by the end of it, I knew much of what it was teaching, and so when someone misquotes it or otherwise teaches something that doesn't jive with the Spirit of God, my spirit discerns it. I'm also able to find answers to life's questions, easily in the Bible and help those who are struggling.

His Word says that He has given us everything that pertains to life and godliness. So, we can be confident that He has the answer and it's found in His Word. Hallelujah!!!!

If you find reading difficult, there are apps that will read the Bible to you.

It's also fine to do other Bible readings while you assimilate a chapter or a book of the Bible. Remember, don't *try* to memorize, just read the chapter or book at least 10 times – 30 is even better – and trust that it is registering in your spirit.

Get the Word in you and watch transformation take place.

Bonus Tips:

- If you need financial transformation – assimilate Proverbs – they were written by the wealthiest man that ever lived.

- Need transformation in your "love walk"? Assimilate 1st John, 2nd John and 3rd John – they're small books so you can read them all in one 30-minute sitting.

- Struggling with depression, setbacks, wrong choices? – Assimilate the Psalms – King David often had the same struggles, but he also knew whom to turn to.

Lastly, if the King James version of the Bible is confusing, try the New Living Translation, but don't abandon the KJV altogether – it's still the best translation…in my humble opinion.

STUDY THE WORD

2 Timothy 2:15

> *Study to shew thyself approved unto God, a workman that needeth not to be ashamed, rightly dividing the word of truth.*

Since all believers have the Holy Spirit, who is the best teacher, the easiest way to study is to just get the Word inside of you (assimilate) so the two can work together. Don't try to understand every passage or memorize verses the first time you read them.

Study tips:

1. Make sure you read the full context. If there is a "therefore, but or and" in the passage, there's more to the context.

2. Ask the Holy Spirit who it was written for, why it was written.

3. Have a concordance, a dictionary (Google) open to make sure you understand each word used. Learn Hebrew and Greek (just kidding), although beneficial, not necessarily realistic.

4. Know and filter your understanding of God's Word through the principles of His Love, Justice, Forgiveness and Grace.

Prayer: Holy Spirit, I set aside my understanding and I make myself a clean slate for you to write *your* wisdom on. Guide me into all truth that I may know Jesus, the power of His resurrection, and hear His voice clearly.

RESTORATION

Luke 4:6

> *(Luke 4:6) "I will give you the glory of these kingdoms and authority over them," the devil said, "because they are mine to give to anyone I please.*

John 12:31

> *"The time for judging this world has come, when Satan, the ruler of this world, will be cast out."*

When Adam and Eve sinned, Satan obtained the dominion of this world, which is why he was able to offer it to Jesus and why Jesus didn't challenge him on that point.

Instead, Jesus said, He wouldn't bow down to Satan. However, in John 12:31, Jesus prophesies what will happen after He is crucified, buried, and risen from the grave.

The power and dominion will be taken from Satan (cast out of the earth), in the same way his authority was taken from him when he was cast out of heaven.

Dominion has been restored to the rightful owners – the sons and daughters of God. Those who are born of His spirit.

Application: Shout AMEN! And remind the devil that he has no dominion and you're not deceived, and will receive back what he stole (tricked you into giving up) and is rightfully yours.

NO DIVISION

Luke 9:49-50 *(NLT)*

> *(49) John said to Jesus, "Master, we saw someone using your name to cast out demons, but we told him to stop because he isn't in our group."*
>
> *(50) But Jesus said, "Don't stop him! Anyone who is not against you is for you."*

I must admit that I've foolishly debated with people who are of a different denomination than myself, and was convicted by this scripture.

So as the Lord reminded and reprimanded me, let me remind you that just because a denomination may do things differently, it doesn't mean it's all wrong.

Let us focus our thoughts, prayers and conversations on how we are alike and how we can reach more people with the Gospel instead of back-biting denominations and each other.

As Jesus said "...I will build my church..." (**Matthew 16:18**), because the "...harvest is great, but the workers are few." (**Matthew 9:37**).

Prayer: Lord, I bridle my tongue so that I do not speak any negative about others doing your work. Lord, I pray for the harvest of souls, and put my hand to the plow to do the work of an evangelist. I declare a 100-fold increase in the Body of Christ and a great understanding among those who do your will. Amen.

COVENANT WITH GOD

Genesis 28:20-22 (NLT)

(20) Then Jacob made this vow: "If God will indeed be with me and protect me on this journey, and if he will provide me with food and clothing,

(21) and if I return safely to my father's home, then the LORD will certainly be my God.

(22) And this memorial pillar I have set up will become a place for worshiping God, and I will present to God a tenth of everything he gives me."

Our God is a covenant making and keeping God. If you need a financial breakthrough, try making a covenant with God that you will live on X amount of money until He says otherwise. And that if He will provide you with the amount you need, that you will use anything above and beyond that amount, to further His Kingdom.

Application: Determine what you need God to do for you, and then make a covenant with God. Remember, you must do your part as God will ALWAYS do His part. You must be faithful, as He is faithful.

It`s better not to vow (or make a covenant) than to vow and not keep it. (Read **Ecclesiastes 5:4-6**)

HARDNESS OF HEART

Mark 3:4-5

> *(4) And he saith unto them, Is it lawful to do good on the sabbath days, or to do evil? to save life, or to kill? But they held their peace.*

> *(5) And when he had looked round about on them with anger, being grieved for the hardness of their hearts, he saith unto the man, Stretch forth thine hand. And he stretched it out: and his hand was restored whole as the other.*

In the above scriptures, Jesus is confronting the religious leaders and legalistic believers who like to pretend they're holy, but inside they're full of criticism, deceit, and vengeful thoughts. Notice also, how when confronted, they simply ignore Jesus? It's because their answers would convict them of their sin, or expose their ignorance of their beliefs. Beliefs that they use to rule over and judge people. Interestingly, the Lord asked me some questions which I couldn't ignore, so I'll ask you them as well.

- Has God ever asked you anything and you ignored Him?
- Are you being reminded constantly about your anger, submission, love, criticism, lying, gossip, sexual sins, etc.?
- Do you pray and ask God to help you in getting rid of these sinful habits and choices?
- Do you feel justified in your sin, because of past or continual wrongs done unto you?
- Do you determine *your* growth and change, by what changes you see in your circumstances, or the people around you?
- Do you find the effort, to be Christian, too hard and so you think about throwing in the proverbial "towel" and living life your own way?

I must admit, I've said in my heart and or done at least one of the things on the list…I won't tell you which ones or at what point in my Christian walk. However, there's only one problem; the scriptures don't give us the luxury of excuses or justification, and once enlightened, going back to a life without God is equally difficult. Trust me, I've tried.

So, what do we do? It's either we have a heart for God (all in), or we harden our heart; which is evil in His sight. A hardened heart only spurs on His anger, which will be released on the children of disobedience at judgement. If you try to live in between, you'll be frustrated. Once again…I've tried.

Revelation 2 and 3 addresses the seven types of churches, one in particular about being lukewarm and another about holding fast (being pure) to the doctrine of Jesus Christ. Each admonishment is followed by "to him that overcomes", followed by a reward. I don't know about you, but I want the rewards of heaven.

Decide today, that **"I'm all in"**. You won't be perfect, but the journey is easier, and the price is worth the reward.

Last question: Are you ready to pay the price of dying to self, serving God and being an overcomer? Let's pray.

Prayer: Lord Jesus, I'll be honest, I don't know all the dark areas, hidden hurts, and sins that need to be cleaned up in my life. I know they exist because circumstances bring them to the surface. Lord, soften and purify my heart that I may overcome the evil one. Work in me, your marvelous power and purge me so that your miracles, signs, and wonders can work through me. Unblock anything that prevents me from laying hands on the sick and casting out demons. I'm never turning back, so guide my way forward. Amen.

WALK IN THE SPIRIT

2 Corinthians 10:1-6

> *(1) Now I Paul myself beseech you by the meekness and gentleness of Christ, who in presence am base among you, but being absent am bold toward you:*
>
> *(2) But I beseech you, that I may not be bold when I am present with that confidence, wherewith I think to be bold against some, which think of us as if we walked according to the flesh.*
>
> *(3) For though we walk in the flesh, we do not war after the flesh:*
>
> *(4) (For the weapons of our warfare are not carnal, but mighty through God to the pulling down of strong holds;)*
>
> *(5) Casting down imaginations, and every high thing that exalteth itself against the knowledge of God, and bringing into captivity every thought to the obedience of Christ;*
>
> *(6) And having in a readiness to revenge all disobedience, when your obedience is fulfilled.*

Although we could talk about many aspects of these scriptures, I want to focus on two types of people that Paul briefly outlines – one that walks in the flesh, and another that is meek and gentle like Christ.

In the context, Paul was giving the Corinthians a warning that if he were to come there in the "flesh", they would receive his wrath for their poor conduct in the faith. However, Paul knows that the Spirit of God that is within him, would pity them and constrain him to be meek and gentle just like Jesus who on the cross said, "Father, forgive them for they know not what they do."

In the first letter to the Corinthians, Paul had already admonished them for their carnal ways (chapter 3) even though they lacked no spiritual gift (chapter 1). By chapter 13, he explains that **the greatest of all the gifts is love**. And this must be true, because **John 3:16** says "for God so loved the world that he gave His only begotten Son."

So, let us also walk in and with the Spirit, giving grace and showing love one to another. No longer being carnal (in the flesh) with envying, strife and divisions. Like the natural, where we wash and put on clothing each day, so it is in the spiritual. It's a daily walk, and we must put on Christ; being clothed in righteousness and washed by His Word.

Prayer: Holy Spirit, cleanse my mind and cover me with truth, faith, love, kindness and peace. Fill me with your wisdom, as I interact today with those who don't know you and are still ruled by the kingdom of darkness. Open my eyes and heart to see how much they mean to you, even in their "lost" state. Give me compassion to reach even just one. I will do this knowing that you are with me, and that I am your ambassador. I will act accordingly, to be found faithful by you. Amen.

STEWARDSHIP

Luke 16:8-10

> *(8) And the lord commended the unjust steward, because he had done wisely: for the children of this world are in their generation wiser than the children of light.*
>
> *(9) And I say unto you, Make to yourselves friends of the mammon of unrighteousness; that, when ye fail, they may receive you into everlasting habitations.*
>
> *(10) He that is faithful in that which is least is faithful also in much: and he that is unjust in the least is unjust also in much.*

I once received a phone call asking about the meaning of this scripture, and my first inner reaction was, "oh boy!" That's because this one had me stumped and I'd been meaning to study it for the past year. As a leader, I should have said, let me meditate on it. But true to human form, I decided to take a shot at the meaning and thankfully, I was only partially inaccurate.

I explained that this was about stewardship (obviously) and how we handle the things of God and that making friends of the "mammon of unrighteousness" meant that we should not burn bridges. Because if we fail, or lose everything, we may need those people. I also explained that the unjust steward was wise because he knew his future and acted accordingly. He put things in order, before he was put out (fired) by his boss.

After I got off the phone, I continued to meditate on the scripture for the rest of the day. When I got home from work, I decided to pull out all my study tools – Holy Spirit, different translations and cross reference scriptures in my study Bible. For the sake of brevity, it's important to note that Jesus tells several short stories in the verses surrounding these verses, so I was accurate on the context of Stewardship…actually hard to miss because verse 1 starts out with "a rich man had a steward" (paraphrased).

In any event, the area where I went astray was in verse 9, "make to yourself friends of the mammon of unrighteousness". It's actually speaking about giving to those who are less fortunate, so that when you are without (when you fail), they will receive you into their homes for the good that you showed them. In Daniel 4, King Nebuchadnezzar had a dream that no one could interpret, except Daniel.

Daniel 4:24-27

(24) This is the interpretation, O king, and this is the decree of the most High, which is come upon my lord the king:

(25) That they shall drive thee from men, and thy dwelling shall be with the beasts of the field, and they shall make thee to eat grass as oxen, and they shall wet thee with the dew of heaven, and seven times shall pass over thee, till thou know that the most High ruleth in the kingdom of men, and giveth it to whomsoever he will.

(26) And whereas they commanded to leave the stump of the tree roots; thy kingdom shall be sure unto thee, after that thou shalt have known that the heavens do rule.

(27) Wherefore, O king, let my counsel be acceptable unto thee, and break off thy sins by righteousness, and thine iniquities by shewing mercy to the poor; if it may be a lengthening of thy tranquillity.

Do you see the parallels? Nebuchadnezzar (the steward) will lose everything because of the decree from the Most High (the rich man in Luke); Nebuchadnezzar is instructed to show mercy to the poor (break off thy sins by righteousness = make friends of the mammon of unrighteousness) so it may be a "lengthening of his tranquillity" (eternal habitation – heaven – will be tranquil). Another way to put it is to "store up your treasures in heaven" (Matthew 6:20).

We are called to be stewards of the grace, and all that God has given us. We are to serve others, even in the smallest way (faithful in little), which will build us into people that God can trust with His work (faithful in much). How we *consistently* handle the things of this world is how we will handle the things of God. The keyword is **consistently**.

Prayer: Holy Spirit, make me wise in my generation that I may be found faithful in all that you've given me. Lead me into habitations of peace and tranquillity for your glory. Amen.

Shout out! A special thank you to my friend, Karen, who asked this question and caused me to study and show myself approved.

NO CONDEMNATION

Romans 8:1-2

> *(1) There is therefore now no condemnation to them which are in Christ Jesus, who walk not after the flesh, but after the Spirit.*
>
> *(2) For the law of the Spirit of life in Christ Jesus hath made me free from the law of sin and death.*

I used to think this only meant that we shouldn't condemn ourselves or that Satan can't condemn us, but then the Lord opened my eyes to another truth found in 2 Corinthians 3, which talks about the ministration of condemnation and the ministration of death written on stones (THE LAW). It says that it has been replaced with the new testament (covenant), and is more glorious because it takes away the veil on our hearts and brings life by the spirit.

The last part of 2 Corinthians 3 contains a verse we've become all too familiar with, but I'm not sure we have fully understood it:

2 Corinthians 3:16-18

> *(16) Nevertheless, when it shall turn to the Lord, the vail shall be taken away.*
>
> *(17) Now the Lord is that Spirit: and where the Spirit of the Lord is, there is liberty.*
>
> *(18) But we all, with open face beholding as in a glass the glory of the Lord, are changed into the same image from glory to glory, even as by the Spirit of the Lord.*

It may seem elementary to you, but the more I grasp this truth, the more I'm set free from sin – anger, lack of love, stubbornness, etc. Are you getting it? No condemnation means we're no longer under the LAW! We've been made FREE by the cross and resurrection from the dead, by Jesus Christ!

If we read Romans 8:1 with the truth in mind, it could read "there is therefore, no law that puts people to death for them that are in Christ" or as Galatians 5:22-23 states:

Galatians 5:22-23

> *(22) But the fruit of the Spirit is love, joy, peace, longsuffering, gentleness, goodness, faith,*
>
> *(23) Meekness, temperance: **against such there is no law.***

Application: Assimilate Romans 5:12 to Romans chapter 8:39 for a complete, detailed picture of what Christ has done. Man! It's good food! Hallelujah!!!!

OVERCOME BY THE WORD

Revelation 12:11

> *And they overcame him by the blood of the Lamb, and by the word of their testimony; and they loved not their lives unto the death.*

I hope you don't get tired of me using the story of Jesus in the wilderness. He is our best example of how to overcome and live victoriously in the will of God. To that end, when **Jesus was tempted** each time, he said, "it is written" and **used the Word to defeat Satan and overcome** the temptation. We too, must develop the habit of confessing the Word. As it is written above, we overcome by the blood and the word of our testimony. If that is the truth, and it is, then I don't know about you, but I'm going to start confessing 24/7/365!!!

David said in **Psalm 119:11** "Thy word have I hid in mine heart, that I might not sin against thee."

John 17:17 says "Sanctify them through thy truth: **thy word** is truth.

Have pain or sickness? No need to "bind and loose" demons. Simply confess/speak His Word, "by his stripes I am healed". Your soul is like the unjust judge, moved by whatever bombards it. **Don't let the enemy out-argue you**. Confess your healing. Confess your wealth. Confess your peace. Confess. Confess. Confess.

Applications:

- Get to know your God, and His Word

- Find truths and speak them at all times. David said, "I will bless the Lord at all times, his praise shall continually be in my mouth."

WISDOM FROM ABOVE

James 3:17-18

> *(17) But the wisdom that is from above is first pure, then peaceable, gentle, and easy to be intreated, full of mercy and good fruits, without partiality, and without hypocrisy.*
>
> *(18) And the fruit of righteousness is sown in peace of them that make peace.*

This passage of scripture is fairly self-explanatory, but not easily accomplished because everything in and around us is opposite to it.

Notice that true wisdom comes from above, and it is first PURE and then PEACEABLE. Yet, from a very young age, we are exposed to activities, movies, images and people who are not pure, nor desire to be. This is especially true in the era of the internet as evidenced by bullying (lack of peace) which is at such a high and pervasive level, legislation had to be introduced to combat it.

If you read the context from which this scripture comes, families and politicians both need to **forget the worldly wisdom and start seeking Wisdom from Above**.

Now that the bad news is out of the way, let's talk about the good news, which is found in the first chapter. It reads as follows:

James 1:5 (GW)

> *If any of you needs wisdom to know what you should do, you should ask God, and he will give it to you. God is generous to everyone and doesn't find fault with them.*

There is no excuse for the poor condition or behaviour of children and people in our societies. We have a God who is willing to give liberally, all the wisdom that we need to solve every problem and every issue that plagues the world.

Bad news again…I can't change the world, but I can allow God to change me. You see, I'm still working on being guided by God's Wisdom (Wisdom from Above) and the peaceable part – Let us pray.

Prayer: Father, as I lead my family and teach your people, I need your wisdom now more than ever. Continue to build me, purify me and fulfill my desire to be peaceable in every encounter with your creation. In my home, with my spouse and children, help me to exemplify your gentleness. Lord, it is my desire to bear fruit worthy of your calling. Work in me, and fill me with your wisdom. Amen.

ACCOUNTABILITY

Matthew 18:14-17

(14) Even so it is not the will of your Father which is in heaven, that one of these little ones should perish.

(15) Moreover, if thy brother shall trespass against thee, go and tell him his fault between thee and him alone: if he shall hear thee, thou hast gained thy brother.

(16) But if he will not hear thee, then take with thee one or two more, that in the mouth of two or three witnesses every word may be established.

*(17) And if he shall neglect to hear them, tell it unto the church: but **if he neglects to hear the church, let him be unto thee as an heathen man and a publican.***

James 3

(13) Who is a wise man and endued with knowledge among you? let him shew out of a good conversation his works with meekness of wisdom.

*(14) But if ye have bitter envying and strife in your hearts, glory not, and **lie not against the truth**.*

Ecclesiastes 4:9-12

(9) Two are better than one; because they have a good reward for their labour.

(10) For if they fall, the one will lift up his fellow: but woe to him that is alone when he falleth; for he hath not another to help him up.

(11) Again, if two lie together, then they have heat: but how can one be warm alone?

(12) And if one prevail against him, two shall withstand him; and a threefold cord is not quickly broken.

One of the most devastating things in the Body of Christ, is that there is little accountability. Rarely, do we submit one to another or become our brother's keeper.

We are quick to be like the world and throw up the "who are you to judge me" banner. Or we dismiss the trials of others with "I've got my own stuff to deal with" mindset.

However, that is not the way of the saints in old times. Their desire was to please God and not man or themselves. They looked out and prayed constantly for each other. They may not have liked correction, but they feared God and knew that the wages of sin was death.

It took me awhile to get my pride out of the way and receive correction from others (still hurts a bit). I'm thankful for God's grace while I grew, and I recommend you be at least willing to receive correction from God and His Word – **lie not against the truth**. Remember, in the final judgment, we will all have to give an account of how we handled the grace of God in our lives. (**2 Corinthians 5:10-11**)

Prayer: Lord Jesus, I pray the Psalm of David – "Search me, O God, and know my heart: try me, and know my thoughts: And see if there be any wicked way in me and lead me in the way everlasting." (Psalm 139:23-24) Holy Spirit, activate the Word in me so I won't sin against my Lord and my God. Amen.

RESISTING THE DEVIL

James 4:7

> *Submit yourselves therefore to God. Resist the devil, and he will flee from you.*

If you've been a Christian for any length of time, you would have invariably heard "resist the devil and he will flee", but rarely do we look at **how**. We also seem to think we can do it in our own strength or by our own willpower. I don't know about you, but if you've ever tried, you probably can testify with me, that eventually your will power wanes. **So how do we resist the devil?**

The first thing the scripture says is, "Submit yourselves therefore to God."

Jesus resisted the devil with the Word when tempted in the wilderness. However, Jesus didn't start reading the Word when he was being tempted, **it was already in him when he needed it**. Also, remember when he was 12 and his parents were looking for him after celebrating the Passover? When they found him, he was in the temple reasoning with the religious teachers (**Luke 2:46**). When his parents admonished him because they were worried, his answer was "didn't you know I had to be about my Father's business?" You see, **Jesus was already submitted to God and when he was in the desert, he was lead by the Holy Spirit, fasting and killing the flesh.**

So, to resist the devil, we must submit to God, have his Word in us, be spirit lead and not controlled by our flesh (earthly emotions).

Prayer: Father I know I can't resist the devil on my own. However, because your Holy Spirit and your Word is within me I know that I am victorious. I submit to your Word, your will and draw close to you. Draw close to me and I know the devil will not be able to stand in your presence or in my life. Amen.

SO, YOU'RE THE MESSIAH?

Luke 23:39-43 *(NLT)*

> *(39) One of the criminals hanging beside him scoffed, "So you're the Messiah, are you? Prove it by saving yourself—and us, too, while you're at it!"*
>
> *(40) But the other criminal protested, "Don't you fear God even when you have been sentenced to die?*
>
> *(41) We deserve to die for our crimes, but this man hasn't done anything wrong."*
>
> *(42) Then he said, "Jesus, remember me when you come into your Kingdom."*
>
> *(43) And Jesus replied, "I assure you, today you will be with me in paradise."*

When I read these verses of scripture, so many thoughts and questions flood my mind. Questions like…

- What would have happened to us if Jesus had been prideful and decided to "prove", to the condemning thief, who He was?

- What if Jesus had replied to the believing thief, "I'm not really the Christ (Messiah), there is no Kingdom or paradise, I'm a fraud and a false prophet."?

- How did the believing thief know that Jesus was the messiah?

Not only do questions enter my mind, but thoughts similar to the condemning thief's saying, Jesus if you are really real, then do such and such, heal so and so, fix this and change that, etc.

However, what I've come to see in the above verses, and in my own life, is that Jesus is merciful and is ***always proving*** who He is. WE

SIMPLY NEED TO BELIEVE MORE, just like the believing thief. If you have a testimony of how He has saved you and brought you through, say a big AMEN!

Today, there are many people in the same state as the first thief; they are sentenced to die, and they don't fear or know God. The scriptures tell us that the whole world has been judged and sentenced to die. It also tells us that it has also been saved by the sacrifice of Jesus on the cross. No one is exempt.

Many people walk around, living, breathing and eating, but there is no "LIFE" in them. Their conversations are death and cursing, their minds and spirits are shrouded in death, pride, arrogance, unbelief, stress, despair and hopelessness.

However, there is a way, ONE WAY, to escape this death sentence and it is through the **life and blood of Jesus Christ the Messiah.**

Few people will argue whether Jesus was a man. Not many will deny him as a great teacher, spiritual leader or even a prophet. The question that is most contentious **and of most importance,** is whether Jesus is the Messiah.

Even the Quran acknowledges Jesus' virgin birth and his prophetic gifting, but it rejects the fact that He is the Son of God and died on the cross and rose from the grave as the saviour for all mankind.

The truth is, Jesus doesn't leave any room for doubt as to who He is.

Luke 22:67:71

> *(67) Art thou the Christ? tell us. And he said unto them, If I tell you, ye will not believe:*
>
> *(68) And if I also ask you, ye will not answer me, nor let me go.*

(69) Hereafter shall the Son of man sit on the right hand of the power of God.

(70) Then said they all, Art thou then the Son of God? And he said unto them, Ye say that I am.

(71) And they said, **What need we any further witness? for we ourselves have heard of his own mouth.**

John 14:6

Jesus saith unto him, I am the way, the truth, and the life: no man cometh unto the Father, but by me.

You either believe or you don't. The choice is yours as God says...

Deuteronomy 30:19

I call heaven and earth to record this day against you, that I have set before you life and death, blessing and cursing: **therefore choose life,** *that both thou and thy seed may live:*

If you are not sure where you stand with God, pray this prayer with belief in your heart.

Prayer: Jesus, I know that I've not been living and believing right. I now believe that you are the Son of God and I want you to be my guide in life and truth. Cleanse me of all my wrongs and hurts. Thank you for dying for me and forgiving me. Amen.

GOD COMMANDS OBEDIENCE

Deuteronomy 4:1-4

> *(1) Now therefore hearken, O Israel, unto the statutes and unto the judgments, which I teach you, for to do them, that ye may live, and go in and possess the land which the Lord God of your fathers giveth you.*

> *(2) Ye shall not add unto the word which I command you, neither shall ye diminish ought from it, that ye may keep the commandments of the Lord your God which I command you.*

> *(3) Your eyes have seen what the Lord did because of Baalpeor: for all the men that followed Baalpeor, the Lord thy God hath destroyed them from among you.*

> *(4) But ye that did cleave unto the Lord your God are alive every one of you this day.*

Although, we are no longer under the law, but under grace, God still commands that we be obedient.

Romans 6:1-2

> *(1) What shall we say then? Shall we continue in sin, that grace may abound?*

> *(2) God forbid. How shall we, that are dead to sin, live any longer therein?*

We are to use the grace and time given here on earth to be transformed into the image of Jesus. Jesus was obedient unto death. Jesus went about doing good and showed compassion. Jesus said that we are to take up our cross and follow him. The 10

Commandments have been wrapped up / summarized into two; (1) Love God and (2) Love one another. In that order.

When I struggle with my "love walk", I head to 1ˢᵗ Corinthians 13 to remind myself what love is, according to God; I also read Matthew 5 (The Beatitudes) and 1ˢᵗ John, 2ⁿᵈ John and 3ʳᵈ John which all speak about love. I guess that's why they call John, the Apostle of Love.

As a believer, it's vital to know the fundamental teachings for living as Christians. I encourage you to be obedient to His Word. Pray for me also; that I will continue to allow God to lead and direct my steps.

James 1:19-22

> *(1) Wherefore, my beloved brethren, let every man be swift to hear, slow to speak, slow to wrath:*
>
> *(20) For the wrath of man worketh not the righteousness of God.*
>
> *(21) Wherefore lay apart all filthiness and superfluity of naughtiness, and receive with meekness the engrafted word, which is able to save your souls.*
>
> *(22) **But be ye doers of the word, and not hearers only, deceiving your own selves.***

I recommend we all read James chapter 1 about 10 times this week and let us move on to perfection in Christ Jesus our Lord. So that when He calls us home, we'll hear those faithful words "well done!"

Prayer: Father, I commit this week to know your ways better and to be obedient to what you've said and taught me through your Word. Teach me how to love as you love, with all wisdom and understanding, that I may not be deceived; either by others or my own desires. Amen.

ARE YOU MOVED?

Nehemiah 8:9 *(NLT)*

> *(9) Then Nehemiah the governor, Ezra the priest and scribe, and the Levites who were interpreting for the people said to them, "Don't mourn or weep on such a day as this! For today is a sacred day before the Lord your God." For the people had all been weeping as they listened to the words of the Law.*

Nehemiah was a prophet, but was enslaved as the cup-bearer of Artaxerxes (Xerxes the Great), the Persian King who had invaded Jerusalem and taken Nehemiah away to Babylon.

In chapter 1, Nehemiah had been paid a visit by some of the Israelites who had returned to Jerusalem. The visiting Israelites reported on how the city was basically in ruins, and Nehemiah wept, fasted (hint, hint) and prayed for many days.

In this chapter, the city has been rebuilt along with the temple, and all the people were gathered for the reading of God's Word as given to them by Moses in Sinai. When the people heard about all the things that they had done wrong and against God according to the law, they were very sorrowful and wept. **They were truly "moved" to repentance**.

Are you moved to repentance when you read God's Word?

Prayer: Father, you know the things I've done against your Word, and I'm truly sorry. I thank you for your grace, so that I can change my ways to honour you. You're a good God, and I'm grateful for the love you've shown me by sending Jesus to teach me how to live in your will. It is in His beautiful and wonderful name I pray. Amen.

A TWO-EDGED SWORD

Acts 2:36-37

> *(36) Therefore, let all the house of Israel know assuredly, that God hath made the same Jesus, whom ye have crucified, both Lord and Christ.*
>
> *(37) Now when they heard this, they were pricked in their heart, and said unto Peter and to the rest of the apostles, Men and brethren, what shall we do?*

I believe in this season, that it is important that we come to a place where the Word becomes a two-edged sword piercing our hearts and cutting away/pruning the things that prevent us from conforming to His will and His ways.

We need to be people who bear fruit. We need to be brought to a place of change.

I don't like to use the "He's coming soon" mantra, but we all have only a limited time here on earth. While we are here, we are instructed and it is God's will that we be conformed to the image of Christ as much as possible.

Prayer: Lord, I am in awe of your grace and mercy towards me. Lord, as I come before your presence, I open my heart to your will and your direction. Mold me and shape me into the person you created me to be. Use my talents and abilities to help others come to know your saving grace. Amen.

HUMBLE THE SOUL

Psalm 35:13

> *But as for me, when they were sick, my clothing was sackcloth:* **I humbled my soul with fasting;** *and my prayer returned into mine own bosom.*

If you're looking to break free of the flesh and walk in the Spirit, you must develop a fasted lifestyle. Notice that it says prayer returned...if your prayer life is lacking fire and answers, ADD FASTING. You already know this favourite scripture of mine...

Matthew 17:19

> *(19) Then came the disciples to Jesus apart, and said, Why could not we cast him out?*

> *(20) And Jesus said unto them,* **Because of your unbelief**: *for verily I say unto you, If ye have faith as a grain of mustard seed, ye shall say unto this mountain, Remove hence to yonder place; and it shall remove; and nothing shall be impossible unto you.*

> *(21) Howbeit* **this kind goeth not out but by prayer and fasting.**

You see, it's because of unbelief that prayers go unanswered. Unbelief comes from the soul (your mind/thoughts), not the Spirit. The Spirit knows and does what God says. The Spirit was with God and created all things.

The Spirit knows that all things are possible with God. It's our soul, imagined fear, faithlessness and doubt, that needs to humble (bow to the truth), and that only happens when you put it under subjection.

1 Corinthians 9:27

(read the whole chapter, it's good food – pun intended)

> *But I keep under my body, and bring it into subjection: lest that by any means, when I have preached to others, I myself should be a castaway.*

I once had delayed a God-instructed 7-day fast. It took me about a year before I finally obeyed the instruction, but when I did, the Lord worked several miracles in me and in my life.

Matthew 6:17

> *(17) But thou, **when** thou fastest, anoint thine head, and wash thy face;*

> *(18) That thou appear not unto men to fast, but unto thy Father which is in secret: and thy Father, which seeth in secret, shall reward thee openly.*

Notice, Jesus doesn't say "if", he says "WHEN you fast" – meaning He expects us to fast. So why don't we fast? Because it's too hard?

Well it is!!!

Your soul and the devil will fight you tooth and nail, in every area of your life, but once you've developed the ability to fast, your soul and the devil's influence will weaken, and you will see victory and growth.

When the nation of Israel faced potential annihilation, by a wicked man named Haman, Esther and the people fasted, and God helped them. There are countless testimonies like that, both ancient and current.

Start fasting and get your own testimony!

Application: Fast often.

In my opinion, a true one-day fast is to not eat food, or drink water for 24 hours.

However, if you have never fasted before, I do not recommend you start out this way.

Also check with your doctor before doing any extended fasting.

Breaking your fast properly is also important.

Some good foods to break a fast with are bananas, nuts, yogurt, raw vegetables and avocado. You can also have non-acidic drinks, fruit juices, vegetable juices and soup to ease your body back into digesting food.

Do not eat everything in sight.

Do not eat spicy foods or drink coffee as your stomach will react negatively.

There are plenty of resources on fasting, so please fast safely.

UNDEFEATABLE SPIRIT

2 Corinthians 11:22-33

(24) Of the Jews five times received I forty stripes save one.

(25) Thrice was I beaten with rods, once was I stoned, thrice I suffered shipwreck, a night and a day I have been in the deep;

(26) In journeyings often, in perils of waters, in perils of robbers, in perils by mine own countrymen, in perils by the heathen, in perils in the city, in perils in the wilderness, in perils in the sea, in perils among false brethren;

I've only pasted a few of the verses here, but I would encourage you to read the entire chapter (verse 1 to 33 – actually read the entire letter).

I want to point out that Paul is explaining, to the Corinthians, what he went through for speaking the truth about Jesus. He didn't write these words to boast; but because there were people, false prophets, ministers, friends and enemies, speaking deception into the ears of the believers.

I want to share and encourage you with an understanding that is so important to our Christian walk. But first, let me tell you how this word came to me.

My mentor was telling me a story and, in the story in a battle, a minister says the words "undefeatable Spirit" and that's when I stopped listening. Not because I was being rude, but because the Lord said, "take note of that". I resumed listening to my mentor and when the meeting was over, I began to meditate on the title of this message "Undefeatable Spirit".

During my driving meditation (no radio, praying in tongues, weaving in an out of traffic (yes, I need prayer), this scripture came to mind:

2 Timothy 4:7

> *I have fought a good fight, I have finished my course, I have kept the faith:*

After all that Paul outlined in 2 Corinthians 11:22-33, how was He able to endure to the end and write "I have finished the race"?

I know you know the answer… because of the Spirit that was in him. **The Undefeatable Spirit of God!** I looked up the word undefeatable and here is how the dictionary defines it:

> *undefeatable = incapable of being defeated or of accepting defeat*

Spoiler alert; that same Spirit is in you!

Romans 8:11

> *But if the Spirit of him that raised up Jesus from the dead dwell in you, he that raised up Christ from the dead shall also quicken your mortal bodies **by his Spirit that dwelleth in you**.*

Romans 8:15

> *For ye have not received the spirit of bondage again to fear; but **ye have received the Spirit of adoption**, whereby we cry, Abba, Father.*

Romans 8:18

> *For I reckon that the sufferings of this present time are not worthy to be compared with the glory which shall be revealed **in** us.*

John 16:33

> These things I have spoken unto you, **that in me ye might have peace**. In the world ye shall have tribulation: but be of good cheer; **I have overcome the world.**

The more we understand the Spirit, the more we'll be able to tap into it and take authority over the devil and have complete victory in every area of our lives and even over the devils in the lives of others. Then life gets really fun! Hallelujah!

I'll leave you with this:

Colossians 1:22-23

> (20) And, **having made peace through the blood of his cross**, by him to reconcile all things unto himself; by him, I say, whether they be things in earth, or things in heaven.
>
> (21) **And you**, that were sometime alienated and enemies in your mind by wicked works, **yet now hath he reconciled**
>
> (22) In the body of his flesh through death, to present you holy and **unblameable** and **unreproveable** in his sight:
>
> (23) **If ye continue in the faith grounded and settled, and be not moved away** from the hope of the gospel, which ye have heard, and which was preached to every creature which is under heaven; whereof I Paul am made a minister;

You see, nothing can separate you from the love of God. The only way you can be moved away is if you quit. Nothing can defeat you because you are in Christ and Christ has overcome the world. The same Holy Spirit that fell on Jesus during his baptism, is the same

Spirit that raised him from the dead. That same Spirit created the entire universe and fell on Peter and the multitude during the day of Pentecost. **And it is the same Spirit that is in you!** Plain and simple! No if, ands, or buts! If it were not so He would have told us. Shout hallelujah!!!!!

Confessions:
- I will be unblameable, because I am undefeatable!
- I will be unreproveable, because I am undefeatable!
- I am unstoppable, because I have an undefeatable Spirit!
- I will never quit because I have an undefeatable Spirit from an unbeatable God!

WALK IN PATIENCE

Ephesians 4:1-3

> *(1) I therefore, the prisoner of the Lord, beseech you that ye walk worthy of the vocation wherewith ye are called,*
>
> *(2) With all lowliness and meekness, with **longsuffering**, forbearing one another in love;*
>
> *(3) Endeavouring to keep the unity of the Spirit in the bond of peace.*

I don't know about you, but I really used to struggle in this area. In fact, I cringe at reading the word they use for patience – longsuffering – and I still have some challenges. Thank God I'm not like I used to be.

Years ago, when both my business and I weren't prospering, and I saw others cheating and they were prospering, I would grow frustrated and angry. It seemed everyone was happy and satisfied, but me. I would lash out with critique and bitterness in my heart at everyone around me; often moving myself out of the will and plan of God for **my life**. I've since apologized to my family.

Then one day, March 8, 2009 to be exact, I was reading Habakkuk and the Lord spoke a glorious revelation into my spirit. First, here is the scripture:

Habakkuk 2:2-3

> *(2) And the Lord answered me, and said, Write the vision, and make it plain upon tables, that he may run that readeth it.*

(3) For the vision is yet for an appointed time, but at the end it shall speak, and not lie: though it tarry, wait for it; because it will surely come, it will not tarry.

Notice the last part, though it tarry…it will not tarry? I said "aha! a contradiction in the Bible. Just kidding, I actually said, Lord there are no contradictions in your Word so what does this mean? And he said:

*The first "tarry" is your expectation and time frame, the second "tarry" is My time frame. Your anger and frustrations stem from your **lack of patience** and perspective in relation to the size of your vision and My timing to make it come to pass.*

I cried, out of relief and thankfulness that God cared enough to tell me and teach me. I then repented of my impatience. Since then, He has worked and continues to work out much of what I had envisioned. Hallelujah!

To top it off, I have much greater peace and I'm not frustrated or envious of others and their prosperity. I just have to wait for the Lord to speak, do what He says and wait for it to come to pass. This book being a testimony to that fact.

If you have a business that needs an income boost, consider James' words:

James 5:7-8

(7) Be patient, therefore, brethren, until the coming of the Lord. Behold, the farmer waits for the precious produce of the soil, being patient about it, until it gets the early and late rains.

(8) You too be patient; strengthen your hearts, for the coming of the Lord is at hand.

If you are sick in your body or needing energy, consider the words of Isaiah

Isaiah 40:31

> *Yet those who wait for the LORD Will gain new strength; They will mount up with wings like eagles, They will run and not get tired, They will walk and not become weary.*

For those who have loved ones that are not yet saved…

Galatians 6:9

> *And let us not lose heart in doing good, for in due time we shall reap if we do not grow weary.*

I've taken the verses out of context, but I wanted to show you this: If you **put your trust in the Lord and "walk" patiently** (meaning do not sit around doing nothing – do something with full confidence in the Lord), God will come through in due season. The something I would recommend you do, is the "four pillars" of building faith – Prayer, Fasting, Worship and the Word.

Prayer: Father, I put my full trust in you today. I will be patient in love and wait upon you in prayer and in all that I do. I believe you will, in your timing, work all things to my good. I thank you for the strength to endure to the very end. Amen.

WALK IN POWER

John 6:1-2

> *(1) After these things Jesus went over the sea of Galilee, which is the sea of Tiberias.*
>
> *(2) And a great multitude followed him, because they saw his miracles which he did on them that were diseased.*

Quick question: How many of your unsaved friends, family, co-workers and acquaintances would inquire of your Jesus if you healed someone of a terminal illness, schizophrenia, depression or blindness?

If you look back on your years of church sermons (I'm looking back 20 years now), what percentage of ministers demonstrated any POWER? Yet, Jesus and the apostles and the early church constantly demonstrated POWER. It wasn't a one-off scenario; it was whenever and wherever they went. Even in Mark 6:5 / Matthew 13:58, where it is recorded that Jesus couldn't perform **many** miracles, he still performed some and healed the sick.

Looking back again, **how consistently is POWER (dominion) being taught** in the church? I don't know about you, but what I've heard is that the gifts are given in measure (as outlined in 1 Corinthians 12)… to one is given… The problem is those scriptures are always taken out of context and many, skip right over **1 Corinthians 12:7 – But the manifestation of the Spirit is given to every man to profit withal.**

In fact, we have many more scriptures that speak to POWER than we do limitation. If you look in 1 Corinthians 1:7, you will see that the Corinthian church came behind (lacked) in no gift. Jesus himself said on several occasions "ask; pray; believe; receive;" – John 14:14/Matthew 18:19/Mark 11:23-24/Matthew 21:22.

Why do you think we're not taught those scriptures? Why don't we see more people (uh um…ministers) walking in power (myself included – **for now**)?

There are many reasons to which I'll point out a few that I'm currently praying on:

1. **Unbelief** = limited prayer and limited **fasting Mark 9:29** – And he said unto them, This kind can come forth by nothing, but by prayer and fasting.
2. **Faithlessness** = limited Word and limited prayer in the Holy Ghost **Jude 1:20** – But ye, beloved, building up yourselves on your most holy faith, praying in the Holy Ghost,
3. **Slothfulness** = not willing to pay the price…time spent with God instead of social media, video games, movies, etc. **2 Chronicles 7:14** – "If my people, which are called by my name, shall humble themselves, and pray, and seek my face, and turn from their wicked ways; then will I hear from heaven, and will forgive their sin, and will heal their land."
4. **Lukewarm** = indifferent about bringing God's Kingdom to the nations – when was the last time we asked "Lord what would you have me to do today?"
   Revelation 3:16 – "So then because thou art lukewarm, and neither cold nor hot, I will spue thee out of my mouth"

God confirms the preaching of His gospel with signs & wonders:

Mark 16:20

> *And they went forth, and preached every where, the Lord working with them, and confirming the word with signs following. Amen.*

Today, the gospel is rarely preached or followed in its purest form, so there isn't any reason for God to confirm it. Today, the Word and power are often mixed with the kingdom of darkness (the world's philosophy and sin).

Last note: Jesus and the early church were prepared spiritually, before the need for a miracle ever presented itself.

Application: If you want to walk in any level of power, whether that be answered prayer, dominion over depression, boldness or even healing the sick, then establish a prayer and fasting regiment and seek the gift giver – GOD. **There is just too much at stake to do anything less than what His Word says.**

WALK IN LOVE

Ephesians 5:1-2

> *(1) Be ye therefore followers of God, as dear children;*

> *(2) And **walk in love**, as Christ also hath loved us, and hath given himself for us an offering and a sacrifice to God for a sweet smelling savour.*

Not sure if you've noticed, but I've been on this WALK thing. I didn't realize there were so many scriptures referring to "our walk" as believers; and I'm only pulling a select few.

Whenever I'm studying and come across one, I make a note and add it to my list of studies. It's important to note that WALK IS AN ACTION word. Equally important to note is that I haven't yet found a scripture that says "go ye sit in a pew". Selah.

In any event, I want to talk about **the walk of love**. In Galatians 5, Paul lists the fruit of the spirit and at the top of the list is Love. In 1 Corinthians 13 Paul says, that out of all the spiritual gifts, love is the greatest and he then describes what love is. In the Book of Matthew, Jesus said that two commandments sum up the entire law and the prophets' teachings:

Matthew 22:37-40

> *(37) Jesus said unto him, Thou shalt **love the Lord** thy God with all thy heart, and with all thy soul, and with all thy mind.*

> *(38) This is the first and great commandment.*

> *(39) And the second is like unto it, Thou shalt **love thy neighbour** as thyself.*

> *(40) On these two commandments hang all the law and the prophets.*

Now I know most of you reading this would say you love God, but what about your neighbour? Here is what the Apostle John says:

1 John 4:20

> *If a man say, I love God, and hateth his brother, he is a liar: for he that loveth not his brother whom he hath seen, how can he love God whom he hath not seen?*

Ouch!!!!

Okay, so now that I've picked myself up off the floor, I'll tell you something I learned several years ago while discussing marriage and love. I learned that real love is less of an emotion than it is a decision and a commitment.

You see emotions can be up and down, but commitment is constant and unwavering.

And so, as it is in the natural, so it is in the spiritual. We must decide to be committed to growing and showing love. Jesus is our example. He could have used His will and rights to take himself down off the cross. However, because He loved us, He took the brutality and torture so that we could be reconciled with God. Let us not use that grace to trodden under foot, the blood of Jesus.

John 15:2

> *Every branch in me that beareth not fruit he taketh away: and every branch that beareth fruit, he purgeth it, that it may bring forth more fruit.*

Let us bear fruit in love. Forgiving one another, making peace in our homes and communities; lest we be cast out of His everlasting presence.

> *(12) This is my commandment, That ye love one another, as I have loved you.*
>
> *(13) Greater love hath no man than this, that a man lay down his life for his friends.*
>
> *(14) Ye are my friends, if ye do whatsoever I command you.*

I always say, it's easier to take a bullet for someone than it is to lay down our pride and our personal desires.

Let's pray that the Lord helps us to truly lay down our lives for the sake of Love, Joy and Peace.

Prayer: Father, I surrender my will and pride to your loving power. Work in me, through your Holy Spirit a new thing, so that I may love as you love. Purge me from all unrighteousness and cleanse me of hidden bitterness and hate. Teach me to truly love my neighbour, brother, co-worker and employer as myself.

WATCH YOUR READINESS

Matthew 24:42-44

> *(42) Watch therefore: for ye know not what hour your Lord doth come.*
>
> *(43) But know this, that if the good man of the house had known in what watch the thief would come, he would have watched, and would not have suffered his house to be broken up.*
>
> *(44) Therefore **be ye also ready**: for in such an hour as ye think not the Son of man cometh.*

I'm not into predicting when the Lord will return, but as I watch the news each evening, I often wonder, could this be the hour?

What I see on the news and hear while listening to the conversations that people have, I really get the sense that no one is really thinking about the end. Even without an understanding of the coming of the Lord and eternity, it seems people believe they'll live forever; as if some miracle anti-aging cream will change the inevitable. Jesus warns us not to be like that. We are to be "woke" and wise. Understanding that He can return at any moment. And when He does, what will He find us doing?

Each day, it's important to act as if it is the day that He comes for His church. He is expecting to find "figs on the tree"; servants who will do the Father's will and bear fruit.

Prayer: Father, teach me by your Holy Spirit to know your will in this season. Show me what I must do to be ready for your Son's return. Help me to bear much more fruit in a world bent on going to hell. Give me the words to speak and the heart to love as you love. I ask this in Jesus' name. Amen.

THE LORD HAS SPOKEN

Jeremiah 1:18-19 (read the whole chapter though)

> *(18) For, behold, I have made thee this day a defenced city, and an iron pillar, and brasen walls against the whole land, against the kings of Judah, against the princes thereof, against the priests thereof, and against the people of the land.*

> *(19) And they shall fight against thee; but they shall not prevail against thee; for I am with thee, saith the Lord, to deliver thee.*

The first chapter of Jeremiah is full of powerful statements, assurances, and instructions from the Lord. It's such an encouraging chapter and makes me feel like I can conquer the world. However, what we must remember is that it's not us that does the conquering but the God in us…and He's an unstoppable force!

His Word never returns void. What He starts, He completes. He knows the end of a thing before it even starts. He knew each and every one of us before we were even formed in our mothers' wombs. He is the great I AM, alpha and omega, beginning and the end.

By His Word, the universe was created. By his sovereignty, it remains. By His authority, kings rule. By His mercy, we become sons and daughters and fellow heirs to His kingdom.

Who is like our God?

Who can compare to his glory?

If He be on our side, we have all that we need.

The Lord has spoken from His throne – "my kingdom will be established in all the earth" – and the best part is we get to be a part of it. HALLELUJAH!

Prayer:

> Our Father, which art in heaven,
> Hallowed be thy Name.
> Thy Kingdom come.
> Thy will be done on earth,
> As it is in heaven.
> Give us this day our daily bread.
> And forgive us our trespasses,
> As we forgive them that trespass against us.
> And lead us not into temptation,
> But deliver us from evil.
> For thine is the kingdom,
> The power, and the glory,
> For ever and ever.
> Amen.

EXERCISE YOUR FAITH

Hebrews 10:23-24, 35-36 / Hebrews 11:6

(23) Let us hold fast the profession of our faith without wavering; (for he is faithful that promised;)

(24) And let us consider one another to provoke unto love and to good works:

(35) Cast not away therefore your confidence, which hath great recompence of reward.

(36) For ye have need of patience, that, after ye have done the will of God, ye might receive the promise.

Hebrews 11:5-6

(5) By faith Enoch was translated that he should not see death; and was not found, because God had translated him: for before his translation he had this testimony, that he pleased God.

(6) But without faith it is impossible to please him: for he that cometh to God must believe that he is, and that he is a rewarder of them that diligently seek him.

Faith is not just a thought or an understanding, it is something that is backed by and requires action. We've all read "faith without works is dead", but what are the works that please God?

Hebrews 11 gives several examples:

- Giving an offering (verse 4)
- Believe and **diligently seek** God (verse 6)
- Obey and do as God instructs (verses 7 & 8)
- Be patient and wait on God – don't get ahead of Him (verse 9)

- Look forward to the future and bless your children (verses 13, 20 & 21)
- Do what is right without fear (verse 24 & 25)
- Expect miracles (verses 28-30)
- Subdue evil (kingdoms) for righteousness sake (verse 33)
- Endure affliction (36, 37 & 38)

The people referenced in the stories didn't have what we have, they only hoped for it. We have the promise and power of the Holy Spirit.

It's time to please God.

Prayer: Father, thank you for the great and precious promise of the Holy Spirit. Help my unbelief as I pray and exercise my faith in a world that is increasingly ashamed of your son, Jesus. Amen.

MORE FRUIT

John 15:1-5

> *(1) I am the true vine, and my Father is the husbandman.*
>
> *(2) Every branch in me that beareth not fruit he taketh away: and every branch that beareth fruit, he purgeth it, that it may bring forth more fruit.*
>
> *(3) Now ye are clean through the word which I have spoken unto you.*
>
> *(4) Abide in me, and I in you. As the branch cannot bear fruit of itself, except it abide in the vine; no more can ye, except ye abide in me.*
>
> *(5) I am the vine, ye are the branches: He that abideth in me, and I in him, the same bringeth forth much fruit: **for without me ye can do nothing**.*

Fairly self-explanatory, but for those who are new to the concept of abiding in Christ, it means to commune in prayer, worship, and reading the Word.

Interestingly, I had actually started writing this before Resurrection Sunday. What I find fascinating, is that the Lord downloaded a whole sermon called The Power of His Resurrection of which He expanded on the whole "abiding in Christ" topic.

The word abide can be substituted with "live in", "remain in" and "continue in" which helps us get a better idea of the depth of commitment required to bear more fruit.

The Lord is looking for people who will pray, fast, worship and read His Word as if it were the very air that they breath. Each day, our actions, interactions, words and thoughts should be centered on

Jesus and the Father's will. **A large part of His will is LOVE and FORGIVENESS**.

Life is too short to waste following TV soap operas, sports standings, worrying about bills and holding grudges. **The true followers of Christ will follow Him.**

Application: Check your schedule and track your activities for a week and see how much you abide in Christ and how much you abide in the things of this world.

I know *I* have some work to do.

MENTAL HEALTH

2 Timothy 1:3-7

> *(3) I thank God, whom I serve from my forefathers with pure conscience, that without ceasing I have remembrance of thee in my prayers night and day;*
>
> *(4) Greatly desiring to see thee, being mindful of thy tears, that I may be filled with joy;*
>
> *(5) When I call to remembrance the unfeigned faith that is in thee, which dwelt first in thy grandmother Lois, and thy mother Eunice; and I am persuaded that in thee also.*
>
> *(6) Wherefore I put thee in remembrance that thou stir up the gift of God, which is in thee by the putting on of my hands.*
>
> *(7) **For God hath not given us the spirit of fear; but of power, and of love, and of a sound mind**.*

I would have quoted the entire chapter, but for the sake of brevity I'll encourage you to read it for yourselves… actually assimilate it…read it a minimum of 10 times!

Let me highlight a few, probably obvious, points. First, this letter is written by Paul, to Timothy as **encouragement**.

In those days there was a lot of persecution, and Paul knew that **at any time a saint somewhere could lose heart** and even their lives.

He didn't want them to fall away because the eternal penalty would be far greater than losing life on earth.

Secondly, I want to highlight verse 3. Paul often started his messages with "I remember/mention you often in my prayers". As saints, we need to do this more and more.

Pray for the strength of our righteous leaders, pray for persecuted Christians, pray for our friends in the Lord. **PRAY, PRAY, PRAY**.

Lastly, I want to mention the state of our nation as it relates to verse 7.

> *For God hath not given us the spirit of fear; but of power, and of love, and of a sound mind*.

My daughter once spent a day and a night downtown with a group of Girl Scouts and she said in their travels she noticed people talking to themselves, giving evil stares, and all the homelessness. She said, although she was with adults and counsellors, it was frightening at times.

It's reported that many of the homeless suffer from mental illness or some form of substance abuse... **they need our prayers**. Even people (including saints) who seem "normal", struggle with depression, doubt, fear, anxiety, migraines, stress and other disease. They too, need prayer and to know the truth and power of verse 7.

My best friend's nephew, who struggled with mental health issues, was shot dead by police. Before I received the call from my friend, I had watched the scene unfold on television and no one knows what really happened.

There were other similar instances a year earlier and it seemed it was becoming an epidemic.

Saints, the enemy's greatest area of attack is the mind.

We need to be praying for a sound mind and reminding ourselves to **STIR UP THE SPIRIT WITHIN US** that we would share this good news and **set the captives free**.

Prayer: Father, I pray for the saints and your servants who are persecuted. I pray that you continue to strengthen them and cause their enemies to be at peace with them. I pray for their protection and power as they take ground for your kingdom. I pray for the saints who struggle with fear and doubt. Put them in their right mind and remind them to pray and stir up the gift of your Holy Spirit that is within them. Father, cleanse our minds with your Word that we may also help those who don't know that you've set all men, women and children free. Amen.

FAMILY

Matthew 3:8-9

> _(8) Bring forth therefore fruits meet for repentance:_
>
> _(9) And think not to say within yourselves, we have Abraham to our father: for I say unto you, that God is able of these stones to raise up children unto Abraham._

Interesting two verses, eh? You're probably wondering, "where does 'family' fit into all of this?"

It all started with a family meeting with my three children. As we each talked about our desires, concerns and areas of improvement, the Lord said, "there is nothing more important to me than family."

After the family meeting was over, I reflected on the family discussion and I began to look for parallels in the Kingdom of God and the Body of Christ. I couldn't really draw on any messages I had heard about family, so I began to meditate on the scriptures and decided to write on the topic. So, let me start with some questions.

- Why did John the Baptist bother to make the reference to children in relation to God and Abraham?
- What was being communicated?
- What does God have to do with Abraham's children?

Well, in the context of Matthew 3, John the Baptist is telling the Pharisees and Sadducees to not think they're safe from judgement because God made promises to Abraham. Just because they are Abraham's descendants doesn't mean they don't have to live holy.

But that's not all God wanted me to write about. God brought me back to Genesis and the Creation of Man and then to the Fall of

Man, Cain, Abel and Seth, the call of Abraham, to Jesus, then to us, and finally, to Revelation.

In the beginning, God created a man in his image. His name was Adam, a **son** of God. He was created to reflect His glory in the earth and God had fellowship with him. Man forfeited the pure fellowship/son-ship through disobedience. As generations pass, God locates Abram & Sarai who, like God, had no son(s)/children on the earth. So, God strikes a pact/covenant with Abraham. Through this covenant, both would get what they wanted; sons/children/heirs on the earth.

However, man's sinful nature proves to be quite an obstacle... getting righteous and holy children on the earth won't be so easy. The children must be righteous, because that is God's nature. It's important because no one on the earth will see God's glory (nature) through sinful beings.

We can't be identified as being apart of God's heritage (family) without righteousness, so God sends an angel to a young maiden named Mary, who by the **Holy Ghost** ,receives in her womb **a new creation,** "a natural child with God's nature". His name, Jesus (Greek form of Joshua, meaning Jehovah is salvation or God saves) and Emmanuel (meaning God with us). **God, through one act, saves and abides with us forever.**

Later on, in the same chapter as quoted above, after Jesus is baptized by John, God speaks;

Matthew 3:17:

> *And lo a voice from heaven, saying, This is my beloved*
> *Son, in whom I am well pleased.*

To make a long story even longer; because of Jesus' obedience (death on the cross) God now unveils the final step in his plan…giving us the same Holy Ghost, so that we too can become a new creation (born again) and thus be holy, as He is holy.

Essentially, we aren't conceived by our heavenly father as Jesus was. We are **adopted into His family** by the Holy Spirit. We take on His nature and name through confession and obedience. Hallelujah!

John 1:12-13

> *(12) But as many as received him, to them gave he power to become the sons of God, even to them that believe on his name:*
>
> *(13) Which were born, not of blood, nor of the will of the flesh, nor of the will of man, but of God.*

1 John 3:9-12

> *(9) Whosoever is born of God doth not commit sin; for his seed remaineth in him: and he cannot sin, because he is born of God.*
>
> *(10) In this the children of God are manifest, and the children of the devil: **whosoever doeth not righteousness is not of God, neither he that loveth not his brother.***
>
> *(11) For this is the message that ye heard from the beginning, that we should love one another.*
>
> *(12) Not as Cain, who was of that wicked one, and slew his brother. And wherefore slew he him? Because his own works were evil, and his brother's righteous.*

1 John 1:3

> *That which we have seen and heard declare we unto you, that ye also may have fellowship with us: and*

truly our fellowship is with the Father, and with his Son Jesus Christ.

In closing: A family encourages one another and cares for one another. In a loving family, there are sacrifices and everyone looks out for one another, and not just for themselves. In a real family, people *want* to spend time with each other and get to know each… fellowship. Godly families don't gossip or take advantage of one another. I'll leave the rest for you all to reflect on what family means to you.

Application: Remember that **we are part of a family and not a religion**. Remember that our actions reflect on the family and God the Father. The love we have for our brothers, sisters, husbands, wives and children is an indication of whether or not **we are a part of God's family.**

YOU ARE VICTORIOUS!

John 16:33

> *These things I have spoken unto you, that in me ye might have peace. In the world ye shall have tribulation: but be of good cheer; I have overcome the world.*

You're probably wondering…"what does this have to do with me being victorious?" Well, let me explain a few things that the Lord explained to me.

The people who allow the stresses and strife of the world to dictate their lives, do not have peace. Lack of peace means there is inner turmoil, struggles and wars.

Contrary to that, if we are not in the world, but in Christ, we have peace. If we are in Christ and He has overcome the world then we, by reason of our **position in Him**, have also overcome…we are victorious!

If we read through the Bible, we will see that God has said in many places, "I have given you victory". But the Israelites still had to go to war to bring the Word of God to pass.

Likewise, Jesus says we will have tribulation, but He has already won the battle in the spiritual realm; we just have to walk it out in the natural. That is why we can be of good cheer and not fear… we are already victorious!

Romans 8:35,37 (read the whole chapter…20 times)

> *(35) Who shall separate us from the love of Christ? shall tribulation, or distress, or persecution, or famine, or nakedness, or peril, or sword?*

*(37) Nay, in all these things **we are more than conquerors** through him that loved us.*

The key is being **in Him** and not in the world.

Ephesians 2:4-6

(4) But God, who is rich in mercy, for his great love wherewith he loved us,

(5) Even when we were dead in sins, hath quickened us together with Christ, (by grace ye are saved;)

(6) And hath raised us up together, and made us sit together in heavenly places in Christ Jesus:

Romans 6:4-6

*(4) Therefore we are buried with him by baptism into death: that like as Christ was raised up from the dead by the glory of the Father, even so we also should walk in **newness of life**.*

(5) For if we have been planted together in the likeness of his death, we shall be also in the likeness of his resurrection:

*(6) Knowing this, that **our old man is crucified with him**, that the body of sin might be destroyed, that henceforth we should not serve sin.*

We need to know that whatever battle or challenge we are facing internally or externally, we've already overcome through the blood and resurrection from the dead, of our Lord Jesus Christ.

Sin and Satan have no more dominion over us…we are victorious when we remain in Jesus!

Prayer: Father, I thank you for your wisdom and grace. I thank you for your son Jesus who took back the dominion that Adam lost in the garden. I declare victory over sin and make Jesus my example of authority, faithfulness, power, and love. Amen.

APRIL FOOLS!

Psalm 14:1-3

> *(1) **The fool hath said in his heart, there is no God**. They are corrupt, they have done abominable works, there is none that doeth good.*

> *(2) The Lord looked down from heaven upon the children of men, to see if there were any that did understand, and seek God.*

> *(3) They are all gone aside, they are all together become filthy: there is none that doeth good, no, not one.*

I'm not sure how the tradition of playing pranks on people got started, but what is really pressing on me today is all those who say "there is no God".

Notice the scripture reads, "said in his heart", which to me means it's not necessarily words, but a mindset or feeling towards God and the things of God.

The Psalmist says that there is none that understand or seek God. They're all going their own way and doing things that God calls filthy or lacking in righteousness.

Proverbs 18:1-2 *(NLT)*

> *(1) Unfriendly people care only about themselves; they lash out at common sense.*

> *(2) Fools have no interest in understanding; they only want to air their own opinions.*

Scientists, evolutionists and atheists ignore common sense and promote their opinions (theories) as fact. They seek and send probes into outer space, but in their hearts is utter darkness.

Archaeologists dig into the depths and darkness of the earth looking for fossil mysteries, but rarely do any seek the deep things and mysteries of God. In the depths of their heart cries a voice, but rather than search and find the truth, they lean on their own understanding and what they can see with their natural eyes. The Apostle Paul wrote this, thousands of years ago:

Romans 1:19-20 *(NLT)*

> *(19) They know the truth about God because he has made it obvious to them.*
>
> *(20) For ever since the world was created, people have seen the earth and sky. Through everything God made, they can clearly see his invisible qualities—his eternal power and divine nature. So they have no excuse for not knowing God.*

The truth is, the more archaeologists dig and scientists probe the natural things, the more the accounts, found in the Bible, are confirmed; the more the truth comes to light and on judgment day, no one will have an excuse.

As believers, it's important to be wise. I've done my research, I've seen Jesus, I've heard the voice of God, and I KNOW HE IS REAL.

The theory of evolution, by Darwin's own definition, has been disproven – Google it. What scientists, of old have believed, they've had to change over time. I've yet to hear any argument that holds up to, or has been able to change the truth found in God's Word. Selah.

Prayer: Father God, I pray on this April Fool's day that many will seek your wisdom and come to know you as you truly are. I pray they will see how short life is and know that eternity is sure. I choose to spend my eternity with you. Show me your ways and by your Holy Spirit I will walk in truth, power, and righteousness all the days of my life. Amen.

ABUSING GRACE

Romans 6:1-2

> *(1) What shall we say then? Shall we continue in sin,
> that grace may abound?*

> *(2) God forbid. How shall we, that are dead to sin, live
> any longer therein?*

To be an effective witness, we need to allow the Spirit of God to have His way so that we do not abuse the grace given to us by God.

Every word, action, and cut-eye, communicates the Spirit that rules in us. So, we must keep in mind (meditate) each day, the words of the scripture, that tell us to let our words be seasoned with salt.

Too much salt and too little salt are equally bad.

To understand how **not** to abuse the grace by sinning willfully, we must understand what is sin in God's eyes. Here is what the apostle James says:

James 4:17 *(read the whole chapter)*

> *Therefore to him that knoweth to do good, and doeth
> it not, to him it is sin.*

Prayer: Father, forgive me for not being obedient to the Word you've given me. I recommit to seek you and change my ways and follow your will. Please do not take your Holy Spirit from me, but lead me in the path of righteousness. Search me and if there is anything in me that you are not pleased with, reveal it to me. I bow before your throne of grace once again and ask for your forgiveness. Amen.

THE IMPORTANCE OF PRAYER AND PRAYING RIGHT

1 John 5:14

> *And this is the confidence that we have in him, that, if we **ask any thing according to his will**, he heareth us:*

Ramadan, which is one of the most holy periods in the Islamic faith, is an annual, 30-day period of prayer, fasting, self-examination, and charity. The reading of the entire Quran is encouraged, and fighting is not allowed. It is a time of increased religious devotion.

My question today is: Have you ever been to a church that did 30 days of prayer and fasting ANNUALLY? I can't say I've heard of any, except one. So, it doesn't surprise me that the Carnegie Endowment for International Peace, a foreign policy think-tank, has determined that Islam is the fastest growing religion in the world.

I'm not here to condemn Islam, but to impress upon you the **importance of prayer**.

In fact, Jesus expected his followers to pray and to pray right. We're not supposed to pray for temporal things, but spiritual prayers – prayers pertaining to the Kingdom of God.

For example, when the disciples asked Jesus to teach them how to pray Jesus replied, "After this manner therefore pray ye: Our Father which art in heaven, Hallowed be thy name. Thy kingdom come, Thy will be done in earth, as it is in heaven." (**Matthew 6:9-10**)

Many times, we pray all kinds of worldly prayers, more money, better jobs, etc., and most often they're not even close to being in God's will. James 4 says, we ask (pray) amiss and thus don't receive from God.

As our first scripture says, we can have confidence in knowing that if we pray in God's will, He will hear us and by extension we will have what we pray for.

If you're not sure how to pray in God's will, look into His Word or pray in the Holy Spirit, because the Holy Spirit will only pray the will of God. **Romans 8:26** says it this way:

Likewise, the Spirit also helpeth our infirmities: for we know not what we should pray for as we ought: but the Spirit itself maketh intercession for us with groanings which cannot be uttered.

If your prayer life is not where you would like it to be, the Apostle Paul has over 80 prayers in the New Testament. All of them are in the will of God, so it's safe to use them verbatim. I'll leave you with three prayers that I believe every Christian should be praying:

1. Ephesians 1:15-23
2. Ephesians 3:14-19
3. 2 Thessalonians 3:1-2

PRIDE

Proverbs 16:18

> _(18) Pride goes before destruction, and haughtiness before a fall._

Annually the LGBTQ2 Community holds their annual "Gay Pride Parade" and I find it quite ironic that they would call it that.

You see, from the beginning of time, pride has been the downfall of God's creation. Satan, the most prideful of all created beings, thought he could take the place of God. In the end, the devil was banished from God's presence and sent to earth with a third of his rebellious followers.

Pride can also come in a subtler form as we see in the Garden of Eden; where Adam and Eve, who didn't consult with God or adhere to His Word, allowed Satan to convince them to eat the forbidden fruit.

Today, the same pride is in the church, where we have all knowledge, but little understanding of the gospel. We don't seek God for his wisdom, which He provides freely and without limit. We go about doing our own thing and living anyway we like, purporting to be Christian.

James 1:5

> _If you need wisdom, ask our generous God, and he will give it to you. He will not rebuke you for asking._

What's worse is we have people encouraging and teaching others to do things which are not permitted by God, just like Satan did in the garden. It's a subtle deception masked in words like, anti-bullying, acceptance and diversity.

21 Yes, they knew God, but they wouldn't worship him as God or even give him thanks. And they began to think up foolish ideas of what God was like. As a result, their minds became dark and confused. 22 Claiming to be wise, they instead became utter fools. 23 And instead of worshiping the glorious, ever-living God, they worshiped idols made to look like mere people and birds and animals and reptiles.

24 So God abandoned them to do whatever shameful things their hearts desired. As a result, they did vile and degrading things with each other's bodies. 25 They traded the truth about God for a lie. So they worshiped and served the things God created instead of the Creator himself, who is worthy of eternal praise! Amen. 26 That is why God abandoned them to their shameful desires. Even the women turned against the natural way to have sex and instead indulged in sex with each other. 27 And the men, instead of having normal sexual relations with women, burned with lust for each other. Men did shameful things with other men, and as a result of this sin, they suffered within themselves the penalty they deserved.

The scriptures are very clear. We are to love one another, but we're also supposed to exhort, rebuke and disciple others **in the truth**. Some may be offended by the scriptures and say those who preach it are homophobic, but what they can't say, is that their homosexual practices are right or natural. Yes, they may have been born with homosexual tendencies, and they're entitled to their choice, but it still doesn't make it right. Besides, nothing in the entire universe behaves that way.

Christians, don't take my strong stance as justification to hate or judge. Rather, use it to show love and patience to anyone else who lacks an understanding of our faith and God.

Prayer: Father, we sin without even knowing and are prideful without understanding. Forgive me Lord, for not seeking your wisdom and being disobedient to your Word. Today I humble myself before your throne and ask that you show me how to share the truth in a loving way. You said that there will be some who will take offence, but that we are to count it a blessing to be persecuted for your name's sake. Father, enlighten all those who read this post and let them know that you are a loving God who makes a way where there seems to be no way. I love you for your truth. Help me to walk in your truth. Amen.

I AM

Exodus 3:13-15

> ***13*** *And Moses said unto God, Behold, when I come unto the children of Israel, and shall say unto them, The God of your fathers hath sent me unto you; and they shall say to me, What is his name? what shall I say unto them?*

> ***14*** *And God said unto Moses, I Am That I Am: and he said, Thus shalt thou say unto the children of Israel, I Am hath sent me unto you.*

> ***15*** *And God said moreover unto Moses, Thus shalt thou say unto the children of Israel, the Lord God of your fathers, the God of Abraham, the God of Isaac, and the God of Jacob, hath sent me unto you: this is my name for ever, and **this is my memorial unto all generations**.*

God through His Word, is revealing who He is, His nature and His promises. Here are some statements He makes:

- I am the one who makes all things new.
- I am the one who promises and never fails.
- I am the one that keeps covenant.
- I am the one living in you to do great and mighty things.
- I am the one who watches over you.
- I am the one who is bringing my Word and my plans to pass.
- I am the one who is building my church. You are my church; a holy habitation.
- I am coming, and I am already here.
- I am the alpha and omega, beginning and the end. I am eternal.
- I am your comforter.

- I am your provider.
- I am the one you can trust.
- I am one that cannot lie.
- I am your healer.
- I am your maker.

Tell the world who I AM.

I AM, THAT I AM.

I AM God. I change not.

I am Yahweh!

YOU'RE CALLED TO LEADERSHIP

Exodus 18:14, 17-18, 21

> **14** And when Moses' father in law saw all that he did to the people, he said, What is this thing that thou doest to the people? why sittest thou thyself alone, and all the people stand by thee from morning unto even?
>
> **17** And Moses' father in law said unto him, The thing that thou doest is not good.
>
> **18** Thou wilt surely wear away, both thou, and this people that is with thee: for this thing is too heavy for thee; thou art not able to perform it thyself alone.
>
> **21** Moreover thou shalt provide out of all the people able men, such as fear God, men of truth, hating covetousness; and place such over them, to be rulers of thousands, and rulers of hundreds, rulers of fifties, and rulers of tens:

The work of God is bigger than any one person.

In the above scripture, Moses' father-in-law, Jethro, noticed that if Moses kept trying to do everything himself he would burn-out, and so Jethro advises Moses to identify leaders and appoint them according to their ability... some over thousands, hundreds, fifties and tens. Moses' role was to take the most important and pressing cases and bring them before God.

Remember Jesus also had twelve close disciples and hundreds of others. When He gave the Great Commission "go and make disciples" (paraphrased), the understanding was that He had already given the twelve apostles everything they needed to complete the mission. He also would send the Holy Spirit to guide and lead them. We have that same gift.

I heard this quote once that says, ***"you cannot teach what you do not know and you cannot lead where you will not go."***

I believe that in the Body of Christ, we're all called to leadership and to bear fruit. Jesus said it this way in **Matthew 13:23**

> *23 But he that received seed into the good ground is he that heareth the word, and understandeth it; which also beareth fruit, and bringeth forth, some an hundredfold, some sixty, some thirty.*

Seek God and enquire of him about who is part of your thirty. Be faithful to the thirty and he will give you the sixty, one hundred and so on.

Prayer: Father, I know you've placed in me your Word and power. Show me those whom you've given me to empower and train up in your Word. Mould me into the leader you've called me to be for your glory. Amen.

CHRIST MATHEMATICS

2 Peter 1:5-8

> *(5) And beside this, giving all diligence, add to your faith virtue; and to virtue knowledge;*
>
> *(6) And to knowledge temperance; and to temperance patience; and to patience godliness;*
>
> *(7) And to godliness brotherly kindness; and to brotherly kindness charity.*
>
> *(8) For if these things be in you, and abound, they make you that ye shall neither be barren nor unfruitful in the knowledge of our Lord Jesus Christ.*

Years ago, for spiritual maturing as a family and ministry, we had started two main study series.

1) The Kingdom of God (Sundays)

2) Spiritual Growth (mid-week Bible Study)

From the second study, on Spiritual Growth, a few things really began to stand out. One key was the importance of an intimate knowledge of our Lord Jesus Christ.

In the above scriptures, several things are listed that lead us into the knowledge of Christ. Paul also wrote, "that I may **know Him** and the power of His resurrection" so there must be something about this knowledge of Christ.

Paul knew the scriptures, having been raised a Pharisee, so I don't think he meant knowing about Christ as many people do. I also did a word study and this word "know" is a very intimate word. May I remind you of the scripture that says, "Adam knew his wife and she conceived" and that God knows every hair on our head.

Today, let us do some mathematics so that we may know our Jesus more intimately, and so that we may bear fruit and 'conceive' spiritual offspring. Let us…

- **ADD VIRTUE** to our faith. In Wikipedia, virtue is described as **moral excellence**

- **ADD KNOWLEDGE** to virtue. Knowledge of His Word – to know and not do, is still not to know

- **ADD TEMPERANCE** to knowledge. Meaning personal restraint or personal moderation and there's even a movement (Google "moderation movement")

- **ADD PATIENCE** to temperance. Patience requires grace and love

- **ADD GODLINESS** to patience. Godliness is allowing your will to be conformed into God's will and thinking eternally not carnally – not thinking what I can get from this world, but rather what I can give of God to this world

- **ADD KINDNESS** to patience. I'm sure we've all experienced someone being unkind to us… so let us do the opposite. I like how it comes after patience – **it will take patience to show kindness**

- **ADD CHARITY (LOVE)** to kindness. Sometimes we can go through the motions of being kind, but doing something out of love or charity (true compassion) is transformational

Prayer: Lord Jesus, grant every saint, believer, Christian, the grace to live today with a mathematical mindset and to ADD to their faith. Father, as we add, I know that you will multiply your blessings upon us and change the circumstances around us, as Paul wrote to the Corinthians – "I have planted, **Apollos watered**; but God gave the increase." Amen.

FASTING

Isaiah 58:6-8

> *(6) Is not this the fast that I have chosen? to lose the bands of wickedness, to undo the heavy burdens, and to let the oppressed go free, and that ye break every yoke?*
>
> *(7) Is it not to deal thy bread to the hungry, and that thou bring the poor that are cast out to thy house? when thou seest the naked, that thou cover him; and that thou hide not thyself from thine own flesh?*
>
> *(8) Then shall thy light break forth as the morning, and thine health shall spring forth speedily: and thy righteousness shall go before thee; the glory of the LORD shall be thy reward.*

I have to admit that lately it's been hard to fast because I hate to waste food and I have three children that always leave leftovers.

However, I want to point out two things: The first is that, when we fast, "the glory of the Lord shall be thy reward" and secondly, we aren't supposed to just "starve" ourselves but are instructed to do something for those in bondage or need.

Remember the man whose son was tormented by a devil? And how the disciples couldn't cast out the demon? Jesus said the disciples' unbelief was the cause, and that fasting and prayer would help them. I encourage you to cultivate a lifestyle of fasting as recorded in **Luke 5 – fast often.**

Application: Pick one day a week to fast. I chose Thursdays as it coincided with our church's weekly Bible study, which made adding the prayer part easier.

BE READY

Matthew 24:44

> *Therefore be ye also ready: for in such an hour as ye think not the Son of man cometh.*

First; even though I've only quoted one scripture, **please read the entire chapter** and reflect on the events that are happening around the world today.

Okay, now that you're scared (tongue in cheek), I want you to know that I'm not trying to be like others who talk about the "end-times". I'm also not trying to imitate other "false prophets" who have tried to predict the end of the world. I'm here to bring to light what they've all somehow missed from **Matthew 24:36** – something Jesus, a true prophet, said himself…

> *But of that day and hour knoweth no man, no, not the angels of heaven, but my Father only*

The fact is, predictions get people all worked up, sells books and gets great TV ratings. Satan loves this because it distracts many people from the point Jesus was trying to make. The point is also the title of this snackable, which is, **BE READY**.

So, I'll leave you with this simple question: **If Jesus were to come in the next hour, are you confident that you're ready?**

Prayer: Father, help me identify where I've been unfaithful and un-prayerful (new word). Remind me to keep watch, in prayer, over my spirit and the life you've placed within me. Forgive me for taking for granted, my days on earth where I haven't been mindful of your return. Keep my mind in perfect peace and not fearful, but faithful until that wonderful day. Amen.

DECLARATIONS OVER OPPRESSION AND DEPRESSION

I was given this prayer by a new friend from Brampton, and thought I'd share it with you all.

I am established in righteousness and I am far from oppression and the enemy will not take my inheritance through depression.

I rule over my oppressors, I rebuke and cast out all spirits of affliction, sorrow and anything attempting to bring me low in the name of Jesus.

Pastor Wallace Vantull

Wallace received these words of encouragement while in prayer and the Lord showed him the following scriptures from which the declarations were formed:

- Isaiah 54:14
- Ezekiel 46:18
- Psalm 14:2
- Psalm 107:39

Here are a few more of my own declarations:

- My mind is in perfect peace because of Jesus.
- God has given me a sound mind through His Spirit.
- I have overcome depression and have wonderful joy.
- Every sad and depressing thought is leaving now!
- Thank you, Lord Jesus, for the victory. Amen!

HOW TO FIND YOUR PURPOSE

Jeremiah 29:11 *(NLT)*

> *For I know the plans I have for you," says the Lord. "They are plans for good and not for disaster, to give you a future and a hope.*

There are over 100 verses in the Bible on purpose and even more books written on the topic, both secular and biblical. However, since I'm a Christian, and since the Lord gave me the following topic last Sunday when I was asked to deliver the message at Antioch Reformation Ministry, I'm going to stick with scripture and what the Lord shared with me on how to find your purpose.

1. **Ask God**
    - He is the one that puts your purpose in you as we see in the above scripture as well as Jeremiah 1:5
    - God never fails and will fulfill his purposes for you if you let him – Psalm 138:8, Romans 8:28, Job 22:21 (too many to list so see **Additional Resource** below)

2. **Passion**
    - Many purposeful and successful people list this in their "story of success"
    - The last moments of Jesus' life are commonly called "His Passion" or the "Passion of Christ". The word in Greek actually means "to suffer" or put another way "something that is a burden". We know also that in the end, Christ fulfilled his purpose on earth and scored the greatest victory for all mankind
    - Find the thing that is heavy on your heart, a burden that you must do; that when you do it, your adrenaline and motivation rise

3. **Decisions**
   - Make careful decisions that take you in the direction of your purpose and keep you in the will of God – Daniel 1:8
   - The best way to make careful decisions is to be lead by the Holy Spirit – Acts 19:21
   - In John 4:4, it says that Jesus *needed* to go through Samaria – why? Because he was lead by the spirit and there were people to impact which leads us to the last point

4. **People**
   - Ultimately your purpose will either need or impact people – John 4:39-42
   - Don't be afraid to connect and share your purpose/vision with people – Habakkuk 2:2
   - To get clarity on all of the above and to move into your purpose, it's important to pray and pray regularly. As often as you make decisions…pray.

Prayer: God, you are the one who gives purpose and therefore, I ask that you reveal to me, through the Spirit, my purpose. Help me to reflect on my past and see how you've been guiding me into my purpose. Show me in my dreams or day visions, whisper in my ear, speak, for your servant is listening. Connect me with those whom you've aligned with my purpose. Show me those who you have purposed for me to impact. Amen.

YOU'RE NOT CHRISTIAN

Acts 11:25-26

> *(25) Then departed Barnabas to Tarsus, for to seek Saul:*
>
> *(26) And when he had found him, he brought him unto Antioch. And it came to pass, that a whole year they assembled themselves with the church and taught much people. And the **disciples were called Christians first in Antioch**.*

While in meditation, the Lord spoke to me these words, "are you sure you're a Christian?" And I thought for a second, if I'm not Christian, what am I?

The Lord then reminded me of the scripture above and that the term Christian wasn't something the disciples called themselves. "Christian" was a derogatory term used by unbelievers in Antioch.

The disciples gladly accepted the intended insult, because it associated them and their character with that of Christ. Something of which they were not ashamed. (Romans 1:16)

But that was then and them, and this is now and me, so I reflected on myself and whether the same could be said of me.

Do others see me as a Christian?

I'm not sure… I know I tell people I am.

But would they come to that conclusion on their own?

Hmmm…

I wanted to be sure, so I searched the scriptures and here are some things that I found:

- Only disciples were called Christians (see above)
- Not all believers are disciples (Acts 5:12-14)
- Christians (disciples) preach the gospel and God honours their preaching with signs and wonders (Acts 5:15-16)
- Christians aren't afraid to suffer and are not ashamed of the gospel (1 Peter 4:16 / Romains 1:16)

GOD CARES AND OUR LIVES MATTER

Colossians 2:2 (NLT)

> *I want them to be encouraged and knit together by strong ties of love. I want them to have complete confidence that they understand God's mysterious plan, which is Christ himself.*

On September 8, 2015, I attended and delivered a message at the funeral of a beautiful young lady who died unexpectedly of "natural causes" at the age of just 23.

What's amazing to me is how this invitation came exactly two weeks after I left full-time employment to pursue the things of God.

As I stood at the lectern, it dawned on me that I was fulfilling my purpose – to reach young people with the truth of God and His Word.

I'm still in awe at how God works. I pray I never lose that child-like wonder; at how God can care so much about His creation, let alone a person like me who has made so many mistakes. And I still do… just ask my mentor.

So, my message is, **GOD CARES** and **OUR LIVES MATTER** to Him and to those around us.

Prayer: Thank you God, for caring and loving me so much that you sent Jesus to pay for my sins. I am in awe of you and know that my life matters to you, and to my family and friends. Use the spirit and life you've placed within me to show your glory. I will forever live in peace and joy because you really care for me. Thank you, Jesus, for loving me. Amen!

10 PROMISES GOD HAS FOR YOU

1. For I know the thoughts that I think toward you, saith the LORD, thoughts of peace, and not of evil, to give you an expected end. **Jeremiah 29:11**

2. I will not leave you comfortless: I will come to you.

3. And I will pray the Father, and he shall give you another Comforter, that he may abide with you forever;

4. …because I live, ye shall live also.

5. **John 16:22** …you have sorrow now, but I will see you again, and your hearts will rejoice, and no one will take your joy from you. (Jesus' words)

6. **Revelation 21:5** And he who was seated on the throne said, "Behold, I am making all things new." Also, he said, "Write this down, for these words are trustworthy and true."

7. **1 Peter 5:6-7** Humble yourselves therefore under the mighty hand of God, that he may exalt you (lift you up) in due time: Casting all your care upon him; for He careth for you.

8. whatsoever things are true, whatsoever things are honest, whatsoever things are just, whatsoever things are pure, whatsoever things are lovely, whatsoever things are of good report; if there be any virtue, and if there be any praise, think on these things.

9. But when the Father sends the Advocate as my representative, that is, the Holy Spirit, he will teach you everything and will remind you of everything I have told you.

10. "I am leaving you with a gift—peace of mind and heart. And the peace I give is a gift the world cannot give. So, don't be troubled or afraid."

GOD EXISTS. I'VE DONE MY RESEARCH!

Many will say, that all philosophies and religions teach the "golden rule" – to be doers of good. But they miss one key thing, what do we do with our sin nature that was passed down from Adam? No matter how hard we try and no matter how many good deeds we do, only Jesus can and did live perfectly, and in the end, paid the price for all of humanity.

> *"Yes, Adam's one sin brings condemnation for everyone, but Christ's one act of righteousness brings a **right relationship with God and new life for everyone**."*
>
> *- Romans 5:18 New Living Translation (NLT)*

I encourage everyone to do their research, get their tough questions answered. **God is not afraid of your doubt or your questions**.

I did my research and I know there is a God that cares.

I did my research and every problem in the world today can/will be solved by and according to scripture.

I did my research and I know that Jesus is the Son of God. Nothing else makes sense when you compile all the historical evidence, archaeological digs, and match it with modern day science.

I thank Jesus every day for the peace, joy, hope, comfort and purpose He has placed in my life. He can do it for you too!

If you are not sure who you can trust for the answers you seek, I can recommend a few good resources, people, fathers, mentors and friends. You can ask all the "crazy" questions you want until you too, can understand the true and living God.

Eternity is on the line; will you answer the call?

Talk with your loved ones, family and friends, and decide together to follow Jesus. It's easier when there is family and unity.

> *"I want them to be encouraged and knit together by strong ties of love. I want them to have complete confidence that they understand God's mysterious plan, which is Christ himself."*
>
> *- Colossians 2:2 New Living Translation (NLT)*

Prayer: Father God, thank you for your truth and life. According to Colossians 2:2, please use me more and more so that many people will come into an understanding of your perfect and mysterious plan, which is Christ Jesus our Lord. Amen

NO OTHER GOSPEL

Galatians 1:8-9

> *(8) But though we, or an angel from heaven, preach any other gospel unto you than that which we have preached unto you, let him be accursed.*
>
> *(9) As we said before, so say I now again, if any man preach any other gospel unto you than that ye have received, let him be accursed.*

Recently my mentor asked me to prepare a teaching on The Apostle. Immediately, the Holy Spirit began to speak and gave me the primary themes for my teaching. At the very top of the list was **the Apostle's role in maintaining the purity of the gospel.**

In this scripture, Paul's statements are weighty and not to be taken lightly (pun intended).

To emphasize the importance of keeping our doctrine pure, he includes angels in the list of those who – if they teach incorrectly – should be accursed.

Not only does he include angels, but Paul makes sure the **seriousness of the matter** is not lost by **making the statement not only once, but TWICE!**

Ladies and gentlemen, if I have taught anything that doesn't line up in God's Word or jive with your spirit, I would advise you to seek God directly and reason-out the scriptures to **ensure your doctrine is pure**.

Application: Study to shew [show] thyself approved unto God, a workman that needeth not to be ashamed, rightly dividing the word of truth. – **2 Timothy 2:15**

BELIEVING GOD
FOR A MIRACLE

Directions for 7 Days of
Prayer and Fasting

- Minimum 30 minutes of prayer each day

- We will be reminding God of His promise to heal – Isaiah 53:5 and 1 Peter 2:21-25

- Because He is the God of Truth and doesn't lie, we'll tell Him we're believing His Word which says "it cannot return unto Him void" – Isaiah 55:10-11

- Give God thanks for being a good God and a loving God who heals and takes care of His people.

- If you can give up something (favourite food, TV program, whatever God puts on your heart) for the next 7 days as a sacrifice, that would be gravy

- The key is building our faith and calling unto God faithfully – 30 minutes minimum each day

- Pick a time where you won't be interrupted by anyone or anything... get rid of your cell phone.

- Daniel fasted and prayed for 21 days, so if you need to repeat this a few times for your miracle to arrive, do it.

DAY 1 – OUR BELIEF

But He was wounded for our transgressions, He was crushed for our wickedness [our sin, our injustice, our wrongdoing]; The punishment [required] for our well-being fell on Him, And by His stripes (wounds) we are healed.

Isaiah 53:5 Amplified Bible (AMP)

He personally carried our sins in His body on the [a]cross [willingly offering Himself on it, as on an altar of sacrifice], so that we might die to sin [becoming immune from the penalty and power of sin] and live for righteousness; for by His wounds you [who believe] have been [b]healed.

1 Peter 2:24 Amplified Bible (AMP)

I truly believe your miracle will happen on the 8th day as a symbol of new beginnings but let us just do our part to watch and pray and allow God to do His part and honour His servants which we all are.

Don't be afraid to make BOLD declarations like "I'm not waiting for the end of the fast, or 8 days. I believe my miracle is taking place right now!"

Lastly, you can also say "Lord, I'm not fully confident, so please help my little faith." As long as it is an honest prayer, God will hear. Let's really connect with God and allow Him to do something to cause our siblings and unbelieving friends to want to know the God that we serve!

It's time and enough is enough!

Read and Meditate: Isaiah 53:5 and 1 Peter 2:21-25

DAY 2 – THE WONDERFUL & POWERFUL NAME OF JESUS

But Peter said, "Silver and gold I do not have; but what I do have I give to you: In the name (authority, power) of Jesus Christ the Nazarene— [begin now to] walk and go on walking!"

Acts 3:6 Amplified Bible (AMP)

We have it on good authority that every knee will bow at the name of Jesus. Everything is subject to Jesus' powerful name.

His name is powerful! His name is greater than disability, greater than cancer, greater than divorce, greater than depression, greater than anything you can name. When we stand clothed in Jesus' righteousness and use the authority that we have been given, He sees to it that the words we utter do not return to us empty. Read, Meditate and Stand on the following scriptures:

- Nothing is impossible with God – Luke 1:37
- Trample on Scorpions – Luke 10:19
- He has given us a name above every other name – Philippians 2:9

Let's Pray with intensity and authority

Lord, you are a big God. You created all things and the whole universe. Healing disease is a small thing for you. Just as your Word says, "nothing is impossible" for you. You said you have given me authority to trample on scorpions, and that in your name, we could do miracles. Right now, in the name of Jesus I evict every disease from my body. It doesn't belong, and it has to go, NOW!

DAY 3 – BUILDING YOUR FAITH

Now faith is the substance of things hoped for, the evidence of things not seen.

Hebrews 11:1 King James Version

Today, please read Hebrews 11 at least three times and ask God to show you the power of faith.

The Triumphs of Faith as stated in Hebrews 11:3 (AMP)

By faith [that is, with an inherent trust and enduring confidence in the power, wisdom and goodness of God] we understand that the worlds (universe, ages) were framed and created [formed, put in order, and equipped for their intended purpose] by the word of God, so that what is seen was not made out of things which are visible.

Let's Pray

Father God, in faith I receive my healing. I believe, right now, that your hand and angels are working and restoring my body to perfect health. I know that nothing is impossible for you. I'm glad that you are my God and that you alone have the power to heal me. You are truly a loving God.

Even if things seem worse today, I'm walking by faith that you are perfecting my health, and, in the end, you will get all the glory.

Lord, thank you for healing me. In Jesus' name. Amen.

DAY 4 – AUTHORITY, DOMINION AND KEYS

God does things in his timing, but we can be like Hezekiah, Moses and Abraham and change the mind of God.

Scriptures

Moses Intercedes for Israel - Exodus 9-14

Abraham Intercedes for Sodom & Gomorrah Lot – Genesis 18:20-25

Hezekiah for his own life – 2 Kings 20:1-10

Jesus gave us the keys to bind and loose – Matthew 16:19

Ask God to tell or give you a sign see 2 Kings 20:8-10

God pointed me to a phrase in 2 Kings 20:5 so that you would believe. God tells Hezekiah, "in 3 days you will get out of bed..." and I believe God is saying to be expecting your miracle when you get up in exactly three days. Hallelujah!

Let's Pray:

Lord, you are a Sovereign God and you can do whatever you want. Like Hezekiah, Lord, remember my love and service in the church and remove this disease from my body. Lord, why should those that don't believe, see my condition and have pity when you can heal me and show them you are the only true and living God? Lord, honour my prayer like you did with Abraham, Moses, and Hezekiah. As Jesus has given me the keys to the kingdom of heaven, I now loose myself from the bonds of sickness and bind up Satan's hand so that he cannot touch my body or my mind. I receive my healing in faith, and through the Blood of Jesus, I will be made whole in 3 days. Amen!

DAY 5 – LET GO & LET GOD

Cast your burden on the LORD *[release it] and He will sustain and uphold you; He will never allow the righteous to be shaken (slip, fall, fail).*

Psalm 55:22 (AMP)

Let go of the fears. Let go of guilt. Let go of doubt. Your condition is not your fault. We live in a broken world and bad things happen to good people.

Scriptures

Hunger after God and His plan - Psalm 42:1

He has a plan for your life – Jeremiah

Know that He is in control – Psalm 46:1

Let's Pray

Lord Jesus I put all fear and guilt at your feet. Father God, you said you have a plan for my life to give me a hope and a future. Father, take control of my life and my body and use it for your glory. As I get to know you more, remove from me every trace of disease, depression, fear and doubt.

DAY 6 – HEALING IN HIS WORD

In Proverbs, it is written that God's Word is life and health to our flesh. We already know that God's Word doesn't return unto Him void (Isaiah 55:11). So today, we want to **focus more on God's Word** and use it like medicine (ingest it) to heal every infirmity. Like any good medicine, it must be taken as directed.

"Many make the mistake of substituting belief in healing for the actual taking of God's medicine – His Word. They say, 'I believe in healing' without actually taking the medicine. What good would it do for you to believe in food if you didn't eat it? You would starve. What good would it do for you to believe in water if you didn't actually drink any? You would die of thirst."

Scriptures

Proverbs 4:20-22 – Take the medicine as directed – until it enters your heart.

Head knowledge won't do. They are going to have to penetrate to your spirit through meditation – attending, hearing, looking, muttering, musing, pondering – to produce healing in your body… instead of wondering whether you have enough faith to be healed, just take the medicine.

Exodus 15:26, Psalm 107:20, Exodus 23:25, Jeremiah 18:1-6

Let's Pray

Lord, I know you are a healing God because your Word says so and you cannot lie. Lord, I speak perfect health into my body. Lord, I speak perfect peace into my mind and soul. Lord, as it was in the beginning, fashion me into your perfect creation. I am as clay in the Potter's hands. Mould me and make me what you want me to be.

DAY 7 – STAND IN AWE
WITH THANKSGIVING

Well, we've made it to the 7th day. Having done all, you can do STAND. Stand on God's Word. Declare His Word. Pray His Word. Believe His Word. Praise His Word. Take Joy in His Word knowing IT IS FINISHED.

> *Remember you are already healed, but Satan goes to and for seeking whom he may deceive and devour so pray in the Spirit on all occasions with all kinds of prayers and requests*
>
> *— Ephesians 6:18a*

But don't ask to be healed – declare you've already been healed!

Your body MUST respond to what has already been declared and settled in the heavens.

Scriptures

> *Ephesians 6:10-18 – Fight against the enemy with all your spiritual weapons – don't quit*

> *Mark 11:24 – Therefore I say unto you, what things so ever ye desire, when ye pray, **believe that ye receive them, and ye shall have them**. [notice you pray, believe and **then you have** – notice also the word SHALL – it is not MAYBE, it is a SURE WORD]*

> *Psalm 42:11 – Why art thou cast down, O my soul? and why art thou disquieted within me? hope thou in God: for I shall yet praise him, who is the health of my countenance, and my God.*

Proverbs 17:22 – A merry heart doeth good like a medicine: but a broken spirit drieth the bones.

Let's Pray

Lord, I have prayed. I've searched your Word and believe that you have healed and delivered me. No matter how I feel, I know you have healed me. I receive my healing and will sleep well tonight. Show me in a dream how you've healed me.

And Lord, as Hezekiah awoke and went to the house of the Lord, I know that I will awake and enter your house tomorrow, singing and dancing with a merry heart in perfected health with no swelling, pain or MS symptoms. I give you thanks in Jesus' mighty and matchless name. Amen.

Tomorrow is a new day! It is Day 8 and 8 is God's number for New Beginnings. Thank Him for your new beginning. It's already begun.

Love you all and I look forward to hearing your testimonies!

www.snackables.ca

www.ingramcontent.com/pod-product-compliance
Lightning Source LLC
Chambersburg PA
CBHW051458050726
47593CB00005B/2130